WRITING
OF WOMEN

ALSO BY PHYLLIS ROSE:

WOMAN OF LETTERS
A Life of Virginia Woolf

PARALLEL LIVES
Five Victorian Marriages

WRITING
OF WOMEN

ESSAYS IN A RENAISSANCE

❖ ❖ ❖

PHYLLIS ROSE

WESLEYAN UNIVERSITY PRESS
Middletown, Connecticut

The author acknowledges the following journals, in which some of these essays were first published, often in slightly different form: the *New York Times Book Review*: "Willa Cather," originally titled "Her Point of View Was Masculine"; "Djuna Barnes," originally titled "The Stature of an Eccentric"; "Colette," originally titled "Having the Best of Both Worlds"; "Margaret Drabble," originally titled "Our Chronicler of Britain"; "Emily Eden," originally titled "Taking Up Where Jane Austen Left Off"; "Miles Franklin," originally titled "Her So-So Career"; the *Washington Post Book World*: "Anne Thackeray Ritchie," originally titled "A Neglected Victorian Life"; "Christina Rossetti," originally titled "Christina Rossetti and Her Goblins"; "Virginia Woolf," originally titled "The Dissolution of a Fragile World"; "Cynthia Ozick and Joyce Carol Oates," originally titled "Oates & Ozick: Essays on Art and Culture"; the *Nation*: "Frida Kahlo," originally titled "Portrait in Blood and Gold"; "Isak Dinesen," originally titled "Dinesen's Voyage Out"; "Simone de Beauvoir," originally titled "De Beauvoir, Adieux"; *Time*: "Diane Arbus," originally titled "Plunge into a Dark World"; the *Yale Review*: first section of "Jean Rhys," originally titled "Jean Rhys in Fact and Fiction"; *The Atlantic*: second section of "Jean Rhys," originally titled "An Obscure Life."

"Fact and Fiction in Biography," originally titled "Biography as Fiction," first appeared in *TriQuarterly* magazine, a publication of Northwestern University, and is reprinted here by permission.

"The Case of Willa Cather," originally titled "Modernism: The Case of Willa Cather," was published in *Modernism Reconsidered*, Harvard English Studies 11, ed. Robert Kiely (Cambridge, Mass., and London: Harvard University Press, 1983).

LIBRARY OF CONGRESS CATALOGING IN PUBLICATION DATA
Rose, Phyllis, 1942–
  Writing of women.

  Includes index.
    1. Women authors—Biography—Addresses, essays,
lectures.   2. Literature—Women authors—History and
criticism—Addresses, essays, lectures.   I. Title.
PN481.R67 1985   809′.89287   [B]   84-23446
ISBN 0-8195-5131-7 (alk. paper)

All inquiries and permission requests should be addressed to the Publisher, Wesleyan University Press, 110 Mt. Vernon Street, Middletown, Connecticut 06457.

Distributed by Harper & Row Publishers, Keystone Industrial Park, Scranton, Pennsylvania 18512.

Manufactured in the United States of America
FIRST EDITION

To Annie

CONTENTS

✦ ✦ ✦

ACKNOWLEDGMENTS

✤ ✤ ✤

I want to acknowledge my gratitude to all the editors with whom I collaborated on the pieces in this book and especially to the editors I am lucky enough to have near home: Joseph W. Reed, Jeannette Hopkins of Wesleyan University Press, and Annie Dillard, to whom this book is dedicated because she is around the corner even when she isn't.

✤ ✤ ✤

We are all prisoners of a rigid conception of what is important and what is not. We anxiously follow what we suppose to be important, while what we suppose to be unimportant wages guerrilla warfare behind our backs, transforming the world without our knowelge and eventually mounting a surprise attack on us.

MILAN KUNDERA,
The Book of Laughter and Forgetting

WRITING
OF WOMEN

INTRODUCTION

✤ ✤ ✤

These pieces are united by two enthusiasms: my enthusiasm for the revolution in literary history by which women have begun to receive their due as writers, and my enthusiasm for biography in what I see as a golden age. The two phenomena are connected. New beliefs require new facts, and the political ferment of the sixties, including the new feminism, began to change the way we look at "fact," at what is worth discussing and what is not, at what is major and what is minor. It began an exciting time of reassessment in literary studies. This book is a product of that time, and the reviews of which it is largely composed were a small part of the process of revaluation which I celebrate.

From one point of view, the contents of this volume are haphazard. From another and I think more interesting point of view, the contents are the result of, and part of, a complex collaboration —the collaboration of authors, publishers, editors, and reviewers in shaping new ideas for the public. Every review contributes to the making of a reputation. You will sometimes hear people say, "A bad review is better than no review at all," and they are right. Whatever they happen to say, whether they are positive or negative, reviews bring a writer to the public's attention.

Between 1975 and 1980, the six volumes of Virginia Woolf's letters were published at a rate of one a year. Every year for six years many of the publications in which books are importantly reviewed in America—the *New York Times Book Review*, the *Washington Post Book World*, the *New Yorker*, *The Atlantic*, the *New York Review of Books*, *The Nation*, the *New Republic*, *Harper's*, *Vogue*, *Ms.*, *Time*, and *Newsweek*, to name some—de-

3

voted space to essays on Virginia Woolf. Beginning in 1977, her diaries started appearing on a yearly basis, and these, too, sometimes in combination with a volume of letters, became occasions for essays. That amounted to quite a media blitz on Virginia Woolf, and it did at least as much to establish her as a major writer as more scholarly discussions.

In academic circles, this deciding that someone is a major writer is called "canon formation." To thorough-going materialists the process of canon formation has nothing to do with innate literary merit and everything to do with the way certain works or authors rehearse the values of the dominant class.* I am sure there are also literary idealists who imagine that nothing but quality is at issue in these genteel battles by which we decide what future generations will read. My own position is somewhere between the two: I believe that values or political beliefs prompt new looks at old writers or sympathetic looks at certain new writers, but, if some essential literary merit is not there, the work will fade from attention with time.

Virginia Woolf provides a fascinating example of how canon formation works. The goad to revaluation was clearly political. Women rediscovered her first and claimed her as a great woman writer. Then she moved into the higher pantheon of the genderless greats. This rediscovery is all the more fascinating because Woolf had been there all along, hardly unknown. But she was, in a sense, not the same writer we see now. She was there in 1950s guise: as a fragile, ethereal woman too otherworldly to live; as a fragile, ethereal novelist of the inner life. She was an important minor writer, useful as an example of subjective fiction (as in, for instance, Erich Auerbach's *Mimesis*).

In order for Virginia Woolf to be seen as a strong writer, literary critics and biographers had first to destroy the image of

---

* For such a Marxist view of canon formation, see Richard Ohmann's essay "The Shaping of a Canon: U. S. Fiction, 1960–1975" in the September 1983 issue of *Critical Inquiry*.

her as the Invalid Lady of Bloomsbury. This need was perceived
and acted upon, independently, by many people. For example
(an example either of uncanny coincidence or historical necessity), in an August 1973 review in *Commentary* of Quentin Bell's
biography of Virginia Woolf, Cynthia Ozick concluded that what
was really needed was a reminder, to counteract the effect of
Bell's book, "that Virginia Woolf was a woman of letters as well
as a patient." I had not yet written *Woman of Letters*, my biography of Woolf, but I had already conceived it, titled it, applied
for and been given a grant to write it under that title, which for
me, as for Cynthia Ozick, stood for a reversal of previous ways of
seeing Virginia Woolf.

It was not as a lyrical novelist or a psychological novelist or an
experimentalist that Woolf became a major writer. It was as a
feminist, the author of *A Room of One's Own*. I and others like
me read Woolf's novels from a slightly different angle—the angle
of her feminism—and found new things in them: a tough-minded-
ness, a criticism of society, which people had not seen before.
We looked at *To the Lighthouse* and saw a different book from
the one which male critics had been seeing for decades—one
written from the point of view of Lily Briscoe, ambivalent about
Mrs. Ramsay, not the familiar celebration of her. Thus, new beliefs brought new attention to Virginia Woolf, and she proved
to be a strong enough writer to sustain it.

In Woolf's case, the process of academic acceptance went along
at about the same time as attention in the media. Academic acceptance—being read in college courses—is necessary if a writer
is to continue to be read from one generation to another. It can
be gauged by the number of courses which include, or are wholly
devoted to, the writer's works. It is connected to the attention
paid a writer by the two major professional conferences for college teachers of literature, the Modern Language Association, and
the more prestigious English Institute. Virginia Woolf was the
subject of an English Institute panel in 1974. But not long be-

fore, when the supervising committee of the English Institute had met to determine the following year's topics and someone suggested Woolf, another professor confidently dismissed her as "too minor." She was passed over in favor of the political poetry of John Gay.

Biographies play a special part in the making and sustaining of literary reputations. Every biography represents a hypothesis —that the subject of the biography is worth reading about. First, the biographer has to be interested enough in a writer to think of doing a book on her. "Interested enough" means really very interested, because a biographer spends years living imaginatively with his or her subject. Once the biographer is convinced (I have seen writers go back and forth on such commitments for months), a publisher has to be convinced. Actually, to talk about "a publisher" hides the number of different people in a publishing house who need convincing about a project's merit: editors, publicity people, promotion people, salespeople. The "publisher" has to convince bookstore buyers that the biography is worth shelf space and magazine and newspaper editors that it's worth review space. Magazine editors have to convince reviewers it's worth their time. If all these jobs of convincing are done well, the biography may get an audience, and as a result of this complicated process, the subject's reputation as a serious writer is enhanced. If people like—let us say—Judith Thurman did not continue to write books about Isak Dinesen, her works—no matter how innately wonderful—would lose their grip on the popular mind, masses of people would cease to read her, and she would be forgotten, a candidate for rediscovery.

So, the making of literary reputations is a collaborative process —a joint testing of hypotheses about value by authors, publishers, editors, reviewers, and readers, as well as college professors. I like the academic term "canon formation." I like its military sound. In my role of book critic, I like to think of myself as a former of canons, a practitioner of canon formation. I would like my essays to be seen as little cannonballs in an assault on an older way of seeing literary history. I hurl, let us say, my piece on Jean Rhys into the battle. I fling Jean Rhys over the wall of the well-defended fortress of "major" writers. I say, "Pay attention to Jean Rhys! She is a wonderful writer. She might even be important. Mention her to your friends, teach her in your courses!" My hope is that after enough of this, literary history will look a little different. After the battle, Parnassus will be shared more equally between men and women.

Like most of us, I have been reading women since I was little. I read the Brontës, Jane Austen, Norah Lofts, Daphne du Maurier. I also read Alexander Dumas, Rudyard Kipling, Thomas B. Costain, and Nicholas Montserrat. I did not much distinguish between the two groups, women and men. For historical novels, Lofts and Costain were tops. For fast-moving and titillating adventure, du Maurier and Montserrat. In other words, when I was growing up, I read women by the bye. I didn't make a point of it.

I graduated from college in 1964, just before what we refer to as "the sixties" began. There were no Women's Studies courses. Even as tokens, women hardly existed in the curriculum. As an English major at Harvard, I encountered only two women on reading lists in all the courses I took: Jane Austen and George Eliot. Jane Austen, indeed, was made so much of that I quickly came to hate her. A model of wit, coolness, and sense, she was (as she was presented to us) a man's idea of what a woman writer should be so as not to be a mere woman writer. I learned in college that Jane Austen wasn't really writing about marriage, as I had thought in high school. She was writing about money, a much more serious subject. As for George Eliot, she was more honored in the breach than the observance. Hers always seemed to be the novel on the reading list which there turned out to be no time to discuss. But even when she *was* discussed, George Eliot seemed to be acceptable because of a supposedly "masculine" mind and style.

The writer who meant the most to me in college—who helped me most in defining my own values and style—was Laurence Sterne: an odd man—a man of sensibility, a novelist who hated plot and who cultivated lapses, ellipses, and blanks in his writing. "Digressions are the very sunshine of the novel," he wrote. Many women writers have liked Sterne. Katherine Anne Porter set herself the task of copying out passages of Sterne in order to master his liquid prose style. Virginia Woolf wrote an appreciative essay about Sterne, to be found in *The Second Common Reader*. In college, when I discovered Sterne, I did not think to myself "Sterne is a feminine writer," because we did not think men could legitimately be feminine, even though women could be, in a good sense, masculine. But looking back, I think I may have been drawn to Sterne because, if he was not "feminine," he was certainly not in a conventional way "masculine." It was no surprise to me that in a *New York Times Book Review* survey of books some contemporary American writers had never been able to finish, John Updike mentioned *Tristram Shandy*.

Gender distinctions frequently used to be hidden behind the terms "major" and "minor." When it came time in graduate school for me to choose a dissertation subject, I had trouble because the writers I was drawn to were not considered important enough to work on. I liked the romantic essayists. I wanted to write on Charles Lamb. "Too minor," an adviser told me. Dorothy Wordsworth? "Too minor." Finally I said, "How about Dickens? Is that major enough for you?" And that's how I came to write my thesis on Dickens.

I began reading women, purposefully and self-consciously, in 1970, when I was twenty-eight. Now here is a problem. I do not know if this happened because I was twenty-eight or because it was 1970. There is something to be said for twenty-eight. There comes a time in your life when you dead end on the search for your identity as something unique. At that point, you start looking around for what connects you to other people, not what distinguishes you alone. For me, this point came when I was twenty-eight. But there is also a lot to be said for the historical moment. *Sexual Politics* was published in 1970. Kate Millett appeared on the cover of *Time* in 1970. In 1970 I began discussing with my friends things (usually bad things) that had happened to us because we were women. Around 1970 we began to think of ourselves as a class. So 1970 will serve nicely to date the swelling impact of the women's movement.

Under its influence, or needing to seek connections with a group, or perhaps for both reasons, I began reading women systematically. And the woman I read most and who meant the most to me was Virginia Woolf. I was not alone. Thousands of women turned to Virginia Woolf at the same time. She became a patron saint of feminism. She also moved into the ranks of "major authors."

Reading Woolf led me to reading other women: Colette, Jean Rhys, Edith Wharton, Kate Chopin, Charlotte Perkins Gilman, Anaïs Nin. I wanted to know what, if anything, was feminine about women writers. I wanted to know what, if anything, "feminine" meant. It didn't seem so naïve a goal then as it seems now. So little had been published that it was possible to cover a lot. And so little had these matters been discussed that it was all exciting. I passed on the names of books I liked to my friends in a spirit of sharing treasure.

In my search for a feminine style and for an explanation of it, I read what I could find on female psychology. I read Karen Horney and Helene Deutsch, but I found what I was looking for in Judith Bardwick's 1971 book, *Psychology of Women*. Bardwick speculated that the major difference between men's and women's personalities was one of differing motives: men are rewarded for and therefore pursue achievement, whereas women are rewarded for and therefore pursue affiliation, ties with other people. I made a connection between Bardwick's formulation and the definition by psychologist David McClelland of differences between masculine and feminine styles on the basis of boundary definition: men prefer geometrical shapes with hard outlines, McClelland discovered, whereas women prefer shapes in which positive and negative interpenetrate—more fluid shapes.* Men like logically ordered arguments, in which the outline is clear, women prefer more dramatically or emotionally ordered exposition. McClelland had used an essay by Virginia Woolf in his testing and discovered that most students, accustomed to a "masculine" style of argument, found her approach maddeningly indirect. I loved that indirection as I loved Sterne's digressions. I began to see a way in which writing style and gender might be connected.

The female style I was discovering and defining for myself seemed in many ways more attractive than the masculine style which aimed at and so often led to achievement. Women seemed more responsive, more expressive, more flexible, more considerate, more iconoclastic and more irreverent than men. But were these traits innately, inevitably, biologically a part of women's nature? Or were they characteristic of any group of people privileged in some ways but excluded from power? Partly with the help of Virginia Woolf, who discussed these issues in *Three Guineas*, I came to think that much of what I valued as female nature was not nature at all but a style created by cultural circumstance and historical experience. I thought this style was valuable. If it prevailed, the world might be a better place. On the other hand, it seemed unlikely to prevail. As women moved into positions of power on an equal basis with men, they would probably lose those lovable traits which were the product of powerlessness. Did that mean that women should abjure power in order to retain their lovable traits?

Primitively, I worked my solitary way through a dilemma which has become perhaps the central issue of contemporary feminism. Do women have a separate nature from men which should be celebrated and perpetuated? Is any difference between men and

* David McClelland, "Wanted: A New Self-Image for Women," in Robert J. Liton, ed., *The Woman in America* (Boston: Houghton Mifflin, 1965).

women culturally produced, irrelevant, and ultimately harmful? Should we aim to integrate women as fully as possible into the structures and institutions of power, whatever the risks to their characters? Or should we aim to cultivate their separateness and turn it into a revolutionary force for change? Classical feminism is integrationist. It aims at giving women equal access to power with men. Radical feminism today is separatist. It aims at change from outside the structures of power. I wouldn't want to argue this issue because I think it's more a question of temperament than anything else. My own temperament, I realized, is classical, not radical. My instinct is to encourage women to go for the power and to hope that the charm and compassion can survive it.

At this point in my intellectual odyssey, I began to get touchy about the word "feminine" or any suggestion that women were intrinsically different from men. I began to lose my enthusiasm for writers who seemed to consider themselves "feminine" in too self-congratulatory a way. Anaïs Nin, for one. When I first read Nin, devouring her journals volume by volume, I found exhilarating the self-conscious dramatization of herself as Woman. After a while I found it cloying. I kept wishing for the external world to reappear. I remember an argument with a friend who took the position that Nin's diaries were the ultimate expression of female nature. I replied that for my money the wit and clarity of Mary Ellmann's *Thinking About Women*—which I happened to be reading at the time—was worth all the feeling in Nin's diaries. This position reflects, I now think, how weary I had grown in how short a time with the identification of women and emotion, women and the inner life, women and nurturing, women and fluidity. I preferred Mary Ellmann's distance and civilization. I had come full circle back to Jane Austen.

A few words about the specific pieces in this collection. They are organized in two groups: pieces about biographies of women and pieces about the work of women writers. Each group is ordered so as to develop certain themes I was working out in these essays (which were written between 1979 and 1984); the literary revaluation of women writers, on the one hand, and on the other, the relationship between fact and fiction in any work or any life.

If I were to sit down and choose nine women to write about, I doubt that Helen Bannerman, the author of *Little Black Sambo*, would come immediately to mind. Nor would Alma Mahler, whose claim on history's attention is that she married three famous men. Nor would Anne Thackeray Ritchie, a most unsatisfactory writer, although apparently a delightful and wonderful person. Most of these subjects were suggested to me. Some—Kahlo, Dinesen, and Arbus—I suggested. But I would not have had this opportunity if other people had not chosen to write books about them. I revel in the serendipity that comes with reviewing: you never know what will be offered you and you are not completely in control. As in ceramics, where you can never quite be sure how a glaze will turn out when fired, so in reviewing: you collaborate with chance. The result is something I might not have set out to create but whose chance-produced pattern and variations, like the highlights and shadows of a glaze, I can enjoy. In this group of nine lives, there are five novelists, a poet, two visual artists, and one superwife, a "muse to genius." I like the fact that these nine represent various strategies by which exceptional women lived their lives. Lest we imagine there is only one way of being female, or even a narrow range to female creativity, think of the contrast between Isak Dinesen's glamorous rebellion against middle-class Danish life and Christina Rossetti's pious conformity. Think of the distance between Rossetti's transformation of her chaste, lifelong love affair with God into erotic poetry and Diane Arbus's deeply interconnected sexual and photographic explorations. The section on biography ends with an essay written for a conference on biography at Vassar College in 1981. It articulates many of my assumptions about the narrating of lives, using feminist biography for some important examples (although some of the innovative biographies it discusses—such as Justin Kaplan's biography of Whitman—are not feminist at all).

The group of ten women writers discussed in the section called "Works" is also the product of a collaboration with chance, although I include several writers who would be at the top of my list in any case: Woolf, Colette, Rhys, Drabble, Ozick, de Beauvoir. A problem here is that one is not always asked to review the best work of an admired author. For example, I was delighted to be asked to write about Margaret Drabble's novel, *The Middle Ground*, but not so delighted when I read the book, far from her best. I had read and loved Jean Rhys's novels, so I asked to review her autobiography, *Smile Please*, which proved a disappointment. Fortunately, I got another chance at Jean Rhys four years later when her letters came out. Fortunately, too, the conventions of reviewing are such that one does not have to spend all one's time discussing the volume at hand. Especially when a particular work seems weak, I prefer to set it in the context of a writer's whole career.

Constraints of the form show up in the pairing of Cynthia Ozick and Joyce Carol Oates, two writers who, as I say in my review, have nothing in common but the fact that they are women and that their last names start with *O*. Clearly, this was an assignment, and my piece takes off from my irritation at an editor's lumping together these two quite different writers because they are women. Serendipity worked delightfully in my favor, however, with Emily Eden, a nineteenth-century novelist I would probably never have read had I not been asked to review her re-issued fiction.

In the section on "Works," the longer essay I've included is on Willa Cather, a writer whose work I love. This essay is a more extended and more indirect exercise in practical canon formation than the reviews, but it's a pragmatic piece nonetheless. It attempts to take Willa Cather out of the category of traditionalists, where she has been relegated, and to move her into the company of modernists. I do this in the belief that Cather is a great writer who has been neglected because critics have not found a way to talk about her work that does justice to her artistic sophistication. To discuss her as a modernist is a beginning.

I end this introduction by anticipating something I will say later: collections of previously published essays are like dinners of leftovers—they may be delicious, but they should be presented with a certain modesty. I offer this collection in all modesty, of which honesty seems to me the best form. I will, I trust, write more in the future about work by women and biographies of women. I collect what I have done so far not because there's so much of it that I'd lose track of it if I didn't. It's what has been done by others since 1970 that is noteworthy. My hope is this collection will focus attention on what has been a kind of renaissance in writing by and about women.

LIVES

WILLA CATHER

✤ ✤ ✤

The trivializing habit of calling biographies by the first names
of their subjects—usually their female subjects—is particularly inappropriate for Willa Cather, who was among the most masculine
(or, in the current phrase, "male-identified") of women writers.
In some ways, it would have been more to the point to call this
book *William: The Life of Willa Cather.* From her high school
days in Red Cloud, Nebraska, in the 1880s until halfway through
her studies at the University of Nebraska, Willa Cather dressed as
a boy, cut her hair like a man's and called herself William Cather.
(Sometimes she added "M.D.") Her friends called her "Willie"
or "Dr. Will." She wanted to be a doctor. She practiced dissection,
scandalizing her conservative hometown with her unfeminine enthusiasms. She taunted her hometown in return, casting herself in
the role of defender of science and experiment, speaking in favor
of vivisection at her high school graduation.

When she became a novelist, Cather frequently and memorably
adopted a male point of view. *My Antonia* and *A Lost Lady* both
have at their emotional cores a man's admiration for a remarkable
woman. Even when she was not writing explicitly from a male
viewpoint, Cather's subjects would conventionally be called more
masculine than feminine. *Death Comes for the Archbishop* por-
trays the imperial spread of Roman Catholicism to the New World
and celebrates the achievements and the spirit of Father Latour,
Cather's fictionalized portrait of Bishop Lamy of Santa Fe. *The
Professor's House* begins by depicting a time of crisis and depression in the life of a history professor at a Middle Western univer-

✤ *Willa: The Life of Willa Cather* (New York: Doubleday, 1983) by Phyllis
C. Robinson.

sity and manages to incorporate the story of the discovery and exploration of Mesa Verde, the ancient Pueblo Indian settlement in Colorado. Her vision was monumental, epic. When she turned to personal relationships, the ground so often worked by women writers, she produced *My Mortal Enemy*, one of the most uncompromising attacks on marriage and living for love ever written.

The great love of Willa Cather's life was for a woman, Isabelle McClung, the daughter of a wealthy Pittsburgh judge. Cather spent five years living in the McClung household, sharing a bedroom with Isabelle while working in Pittsburgh as a managing editor and high school teacher. But she and Isabelle McClung could not spend their lives together. Samuel McClung would not allow it, and his daughter depended on his money. When the thirty-two-year-old Cather moved to New York in 1906 to work for the lively and important *McClure's Magazine* (she eventually became its managing editor), Isabelle McClung did not go with her. Two years later, Cather began sharing an apartment in New York with Edith Lewis, who also worked in publishing, and the two women lived and traveled together until Cather's death in 1947. Phyllis C. Robinson is the first biographer of Willa Cather to acknowledge explicitly that she was a lesbian. But she does it so blandly that the fact hardly carries any weight.

Good biographies of Willa Cather exist. There is one by E. K. Brown that was completed by Leon Edel* and another, more recent, with better discussions of her work, by James Woodress.† A new biography—and one is needed—must address frankly and fully the complex subject of Cather's sexual identity and its relationship to her work. Did she write from the male point of view in order to hide her own attraction to women behind a male mask, or because she felt more like a man than a woman? Or for other reasons entirely? Marguerite Yourcenar, whose work in some interesting ways resembles Cather's, remarked on the impossibility

---

Willa Cather: A Critical Biography (New York: Knopf, 1953).
† *Willa Cather: Her Life and Art* (New York: Pegasus, 1970).

of making a woman the axis for a novel such as her *Hadrian's Memoirs*. A woman's life is too limited or too secret, Yourcenar thought. If she had ascribed to a woman the kind of wide-ranging meditations she assigned to Hadrian, people would have said she hadn't created a convincing woman. This is the kind of problem someone writing seriously about Willa Cather must confront. Phyllis Robinson is simply not up to it. She writes, "If [Cather] seems to be saying, 'Why can't a woman be more like a man?' that may be precisely what she meant." Robinson asks some good questions but answers them lamely: "Would *My Ántonia*, for one, or *A Lost Lady* have been better books if they had been told from the point of view of women instead of men? Perhaps, but then they would not have been the books we know." Sometimes the answers are combined with a particularly disingenuous rhetorical ploy— raising a possibility only to dismiss it as insufficiently documented. In the discussion of Cather's seemingly gratuitous attack in print on the Harvard legal historian Roscoe Pound, with whose sister she was in love in her Red Cloud days, Robinson asks, "What had Roscoe Pound done to cause her outburst?" In response to this reasonable question, she speculates wildly. "Perhaps he called the friendship unnatural and his sister's friend perverse. He may even have used the term 'lesbian' to describe her. We do not know." I do not mind the wild speculation so much as the prim disavowal in the name of scrupulous factuality. The thing has been summoned up. The writer must take responsibility for it.

A biography of Willa Cather demands speculation, intuition, and a willingness to go out on a limb, because there is relatively little documentary material. Cather was an intensely private person who retrieved and burned as many of her letters as she could. After her death, Edith Lewis continued this work of concealment. The letters to McClung and Lewis are gone. One part of the correspondence that escaped the conflagration was that with a Boston woman, Elizabeth (Elsie) Sergeant, and Robinson relies heavily on these letters, giving *Willa*, in the years they cover, somewhat more texture than previous biographies. But elsewhere the book is too timid. A section called "A Good First Mate" discusses Edith Lewis's role in Cather's life. "Their life together was undoubtedly a marriage in every sense," Robinson writes, but she does not go on to explore the ways in which their relationship was a marriage. She cites Elizabeth Sergeant's description of Edith Lewis as a good first mate, helping the captain steer the ship through the rocks with a lot of unacknowledged work. "It is an apt description of Edith's role in Willa's life," she says, "but it is not the whole story." What is the whole story? As Robinson might put it, "We do not know."

It is time to remove some of the pink and blue from our image of the apple-cheeked and prairie-blue-eyed Willa Cather. This writer we think of as Middle Western spent most of her life in the East. She chose to be a New Yorker. She was the hard-driving editor of a successful magazine and didn't start writing fiction full time until she was forty. Her literary ties were to Europe. The girl next door of American letters hated small-town America, rejected heterosexuality, and distrusted the family as the enemy of art. It is time to establish Willa Cather's complexity and her stature as a writer. The job is open for another biographer.

FRIDA KAHLO

✤ ✤ ✤

Hayden Herrera is forthright and unpretentious in her telling of
the life of the painter Frida Kahlo. But then, Kahlo's was a life so
colorful as to require no heightening. She was born in 1907 in
Mexico City of Spanish-Indian heritage on her mother's side and
Hungarian-Jewish on her father's. When she was eighteen, a bus
she was riding on was rammed by a trolley. A broken handrail
from the trolley entered her body on her left side, at waist level,
and emerged between her legs. Somehow, the accident removed
all her clothes. She lay in the street naked, skewered by an iron
rod, covered in blood and in gold—someone traveling on the bus
had been carrying gold paint. When life provides images like this,
who needs pyrotechnics in biography?

After the accident, Kahlo endured continuous fatigue as well as
pain in her spine and right leg. Her spinal column and her pelvis
had each been broken in three places, her leg—already damaged
from childhood polio—was broken in eight places and her right
foot crushed. She had thirty-two operations on her back before
her death in 1954. "She lived dying," a friend said. But that does
not suggest the joy with which she lived, the energy, passion, humor and gallant morbidity. She did not merely live with death, she
danced with it. Mexicans still celebrate the Day of the Dead by
playing with skeleton toys, and Kahlo had her own games. For
many years a skeleton lay on top of the canopy of the bed in which
she slept.

The role of the heroic sufferer, death's playmate, for whom
death gives an edge to the enjoyment of life, became central to her

✤ *Frida: A Biography of Frida Kahlo* (New York: Harper & Row, 1983) by
Hayden Herrera.

self-image. Although her paintings often depict her physical fracture and pain, they are never self-pitying. In *The Broken Column*, her body is riven down the middle, studded with nails, and held together by an orthopedic corset; her spine is a shattered classical column, but her proud bearing and queenly gaze signal her determination to endure—with style.

In 1929, Kahlo married Diego Rivera, Mexico's most famous artist. She had started painting after the accident, to amuse herself during the months of recuperation in bed. Eventually, curious to know if she had a chance for a career as a painter, she took her work to Rivera. He thought she had talent. He also thought she was enchanting. She certainly was striking, with dark eyebrows that joined over her nose. Rivera, twice-divorced, was forty-two. She was twenty-two. At three hundred pounds, he was so obese his underwear had to be specially made. She was delicate and small. They were a memorably incongruous couple—an elephant matched with a dove, her parents said. His sloppiness stood out all the more when Kahlo was dressed, as she often was, in a vivid floor-length skirt and embroidered blouse such as the women of Tehuantepec wore. (The peasant dress was intended to show Kahlo's allegiance to native Mexican culture, but it also served to hide her withered right leg.)

However incongruous they looked, Kahlo and Rivera shared wit, a love of art, a hatred of the bourgeoisie, and sexual energy (not always directed toward each other). For many years they lived in separate houses Juan O'Gorman designed for them in the San Angel section of Mexico City—hers blue, his pink, the two connected by a bridge at the topmost level. Their lives were like that, flagrantly independent but solidly joined. Despite his fat, sloppiness, and frog face, Rivera's sexual magnetism was considerable, and his bed became part of the trip for many American *turistas*. But Kahlo was hardly inactive—with women as well as men. When Rivera hurt her by sleeping with her sister, her retaliation was inspired. Kicking him right in his politics, she had an affair with Trotsky who had come to Mexico in exile in 1937. Her list of lovers shows a heady mixture of art and politics: Trotsky had been preceded by the sculptor Isamu Noguchi.

Kahlo and Rivera were at the center of cultural and political life in Mexico at a particularly exciting time. The Mexican Revolution had begun in 1910, the year Kahlo—as much from patriotism as vanity—preferred to 1907 as the year of her birth. By the 1920s, Mexican art was flourishing. The great muralists—Siqueiros and Orozco, as well as Rivera—were painting monumental public spaces, in an effort to bring art to the people. They repudiated easel painting as elitist. Pre-Columbian art, which had no particular cachet before the Revolution, now became prized as nobly, quintessentially Mexican. (Rivera spent most of his money amassing one of Mexico's finest collections of pre-Columbian art.)

For Kahlo and Rivera, *Mexicanidad* meant Communism. He was the secretary of the Mexican Communist Party, and the typical 1930s collision between art and politics was more than typically tumultuous in his case. In 1929, Rivera began his great mural on the stairway of the National Palace, depicting all of Mexican history from a Marxist point of view. The work was political dynamite. Conservatives were outraged by the disrespectful portraits of some recent Mexican presidents and the caricatures of evil capitalists. Communists were equally outraged that Rivera had accepted a commission from the government to paint the National Palace. They expelled him from the party. Tired of taking a beating from both sides, the artist went with his wife to "Gringolandia," where he spent four years painting heroic celebrations of labor and technology in San Francisco, Detroit, and New York City, until his portrait of Lenin on the walls of Rockefeller Center led the Rockefellers to pay him his fee, dismiss him, and destroy his mural.

While Rivera was painting the pageant of labor on the grandest scale possible, Frida Kahlo was also painting, intimately and privately. Most of her two hundred-odd paintings are self-portraits. They are painted on metal and masonite panels, or canvases never larger than the despised elitist size that fit on an easel. The irony is more apparent than real: an invalid cannot be expected to paint murals. Kahlo was forced to spend not just days, but months, lying on her back. Most of her paintings were small enough to have been worked on in bed. Many of them were inspired by *retablos*, small votive paintings which commemorate a disaster or a deliverance.

Although her work belongs in the tradition of naïve painting—the drawing is innocently painstaking, the colors odd, perspective awkward—Kahlo was knowledgeable about art. She was associated with artists, critics, and art historians. She admired Piero della Francesca, Grünewald, Bosch, and Klee, as well as Gauguin and Rousseau. "It was not provincialism," writes Herrera, "that made Frida borrow folk art modes." It was part of her *Mexicanidad*, which was for her "a style, a political stance, and a psychological support," helping to cover her psychic wounds as her Tehuana skirt covered her withered leg.

Herrera's excellence as Kahlo's biographer emerges in her treatment of the paintings, skillfully placed in the context of Mexican art. She is able to point out the similarity between the striking and somewhat horrifying image in *My Birth*—a woman whose body is covered from the waist up gives birth to an adult-sized Kahlo—and an Aztec stone sculpture of a squatting woman giving birth to a man with a full-grown head. In *My Nurse and I*, Kahlo, again an infant with an outsized head, suckles the breast of an idol-faced Indian whose milk glands are painted on the outside of her breast. Herrera can tell us that in ceramic sculptures of the first century A.D. from Jalisco, the glands of nursing women are represented in a plantlike pattern on their breasts. *The Deceased Dimas*, a painting of a dead child, is located in a tradition of post-mortem portraiture going back to colonial times. In this way, much that would otherwise seem bizarre or grotesque in Kahlo's imagery is shown as her reworking of her visual heritage.

Kahlo was as attentive to the details of her daily life as to those of her painted works. She dressed with as much care as some peo-

ple take to write a paragraph, thoughtfully choosing her daily display of jewelry (from a fantastic collection Rivera gave her) and
occasionally even sewing an extra bow on her outfit for effect. She
decorated Rivera's lunch basket with flowers and meticulously arranged the fruit on their table. In her later years, when she taught,
she brought her students into her home, and the stuff of her household became the subject of their still lifes. She set them painting
murals for the local *pulquería*, and they went on to paint the local
washerwomen's workhouse. For Kahlo, in all ways, the line between life and art was thin indeed, so that the task of her biographer is to "read" the autobiography she has already provided
in her art.

Even *The Two Fridas*, one of Kahlo's best-known paintings,
benefits from biographical explication. In this double self-portrait,
one Frida, dressed as a Tehuana, sits on a bench holding the
hand of another Frida, in Victorian dress, whose arteries and
wounded heart are painted—in Kahlo-vision—outside her body.
The heart of the Tehuana Frida, who holds a miniature portrait of
Rivera on her lap, is intact. The wounded Frida bleeds over her
white skirt. With a surgical clamp, she tries to stem the flow of her
blood. Viewed cold, it is a striking image of duality, but it certainly helps to know that when she was painting *The Two Fridas*,
Kahlo was in despair about her separation from her husband.
(They were divorced in 1939 but remarried the following year.)
The Tehuana Frida is the one Diego loved, and she is comforting
the one he loves no longer. Although André Breton tried to claim
Kahlo as a surrealist, and although Kahlo herself took advantage
of the vogue for surrealism to market her work, her strange imagery is readable if you know her life. It does not proceed from an
obscure unconscious. (She and Rivera eventually came to see
surrealism as a decadent European attempt to regain contact with
sources of vitality that had never been lost in Mexico.) "I never
painted dreams," she wrote. "I painted my own reality."

Herrera belongs to a naïve tradition of biography as Kahlo belongs to a naïve tradition of painting. Her discussion of Kahlo's work is strong; less so is her historical analysis and psychological inquiry. She doesn't probe deeply. But then, she doesn't need to: the blood—and gold—of this life are right on the surface. She is "naïve," too, in her handling of some biographical materials, quoting letters at length but making little effort to incorporate them into the text. But again, I didn't mind much. The effect, like that of Kahlo's naïveté, is often captivating. I enjoyed even the signatures on some of the Riveras' letters to each other, as when Diego signs himself "Your No. 1 Toad-Frog." Nor would I give up their expressions of affection: "Really without you [he wrote to Frida] this life does not matter to me more than approximately two peanuts at most."

Kahlo's writing was as colorful as everything else she made out of life. From Paris, where she had a show in 1939, she wrote in English to her lover Nikolas Muray in New York: "I rather sit on the floor in the market of Toluca and sell tortillas, than to have anything to do with these 'artistic' bitches of Paris. They sit for hours on the 'cafes' warming their precious behinds, and talk without stopping about 'culture' 'art' 'revolution' and so forth thinking themselves the gods of the world. . . . Gee weez! It was worthwhile to come here only to see why Europe is rottening."

To the credit of North American art-lovers, Kahlo's show in New York in 1938 was a great success. She was not a success in Paris. The French, Herrera suggests, were too nationalistic to be interested in the work of such an exotic foreigner and too chauvinistic to be much interested in the work of a woman. But the thirties seem to have marked the high point of North America's cultural interest in Mexico, until fairly recently. (I am thinking of the current interest in Latin American writing.) Our passion for reading about *la vie de bohème* has been expended to a large extent on Bloomsbury and on American expatriates in Paris. If we need to participate, however vicariously, in bohemian verve—and it seems we do—why should we know so much about the love life of Lytton Strachey and have been so long deprived of information about the infinitely juicier love life of the Riveras? Why didn't we know that Mexico offered us as good a bohemia as any in Europe? Because our cultural interests—like our political ties—are linguistically and not geographically determined? Rivera saw the connection between the pyramids of the Yucatán and the skyscrapers of New York and dreamed of the growth of a truly pan-American culture. It hasn't happened yet.

How important an artist was Frida Kahlo? Although the strength of her work is undeniable, her paintings are small in size. Her output was limited. Her subject matter is personal. By the usual standards, she is not a major painter. But one exciting result of the new feminism, and particularly of feminist biography, has been to make us rethink questions about what is major and what is minor. As with Jean Strouse's biography of Alice James, there is nothing particularly feminist about Hayden Herrera's biography of Kahlo—except the fact that she wrote it.

DJUNA BARNES

✤ ✤ ✤

Djuna Barnes, whose best-known novel, *Nightwood*, was published in 1936, died in 1982 at the age of ninety. Fragile, ill, unproductive, she had clung for many years to a minimal life in the tiny Greenwich Village apartment she had inhabited since returning to America in 1940. In Europe she had been a glamorous member of the expatriate community—fashionably talented, enigmatic, and homosexual. In Paris she was part of the legendary group of women around the heiress Natalie Barney. In England she was a member of Peggy Guggenheim's entourage. But back in New York, she rarely left her apartment. Her great love affair—with Thelma Wood, an American sculptor—was long over; she had written *Nightwood* about it. She published one other major work, *The Antiphon*, a verse drama, in 1958. E. E. Cummings, who lived across from Barnes in the Village, would shout out his window from time to time, "Are ya still alive, Djuna?" Even now, it's a good question. Is she still alive as a writer?

This eccentric biography of an eccentric literary figure is unlikely to win her new readers. Nor does it settle any questions about Barnes's stature and the viability of her work. Andrew Field is convinced that Djuna Barnes is "a major writer of our time," but his placing her in a category with James Joyce and T. S. Eliot merely makes us chortle. Joyce, Eliot, and Barnes? It's as unconvincing a group as Tom, Dick, and Francis. "Joyce gave a new form to the novel. Eliot gave a new voice to English poetry," explains Field. "Barnes was comparatively disadvantaged because her main narrative cargo was her rather singular family experi-

✤ *Djuna: The Life and Times of Djuna Barnes* (New York: Putnam's, 1983) by Andrew Field.

ence . . . and also because she was a woman and a most unusual
sort of woman at that." Joyce and Eliot are ascribed achievements;
Barnes is given an excuse.

Field, the biographer also of Nabokov, is only the most recent
of a distinguished line of literary men who have made excuses for
Djuna Barnes. T. S. Eliot, in his role of editor at Faber & Faber,
was responsible for getting *Nightwood* published in England, and
the introduction he wrote for it, praising the novel's poetic taut-
ness, helped ensure its eventual publication in America and a continuing sale, for fifty years, of several thousand copies a year. Dy-
lan Thomas wrote of *Nightwood*, "It isn't a lah-de-dah prose poem"
and called it "one of the three great prose books ever written by
a woman." Almost everyone who praises Djuna Barnes praises her
as a "woman writer." She was a dancing dog of the twenties, expatriate America's favorite "woman writer." People responded to
the intensity and promise of her work but also to her charm. Joyce
gave her a signed copy of *Ulysses*. She was the only person in Paris
with the nerve to call him "Jim" to his face, and presumably he
liked that. Eliot, too, enjoyed her company. It was said he lost his
English stiffness of manner only in her presence, and he kept her
framed photograph in his office at Faber's—along with that of
Groucho Marx. Recent feminist biography has been challenging
in exciting ways our accepted notions of major and minor. But the
fact that an artist has been underappreciated does not mean her
work is major. Field offers us another trio as incongruous as Eliot,
Joyce, and Barnes. "Colette, Woolf, and Barnes," he tells us, "might
in time sit more comfortably on the Parnassus of their time with
Proust, Eliot, and Joyce, than many writers of the time whose
works already show clear signs of becoming period pieces." For
the resolution of a chord beginning with Colette and Woolf, my
own choice would be Gertrude Stein; but Stein, living and writing
in Paris at the same time as Djuna Barnes, figures in this book only
as someone with whom Barnes did not get along. This partisan-
ship, this absence of perspective, produces some outrageous state-

ments, like the assertion that no woman writer has ever had a better sense of humor than Djuna Barnes or the judgment that "the
Barnes oeuvre may be said to be one of the best instances of deep
autoanalysis outside the Freudian canon in modern English literature."

In the face of such overstatements, I remain an agnostic. Djuna
Barnes may perhaps be a great and unjustly neglected writer, but
it will take another book to prove it to me. Field quotes at length
from Barnes's novel *Ryder* and then says: "That passage—it is
Barnes at her best, though there are many other passages from
Nightwood and *The Antiphon* which might have been selected instead—should be full and sufficient proof of the place of Djuna
Barnes in modern literature, even though many histories give her
only a line or two." The passage? Here is some of it: "The horses
whinnied as he touched their fetlocks, and the kine were shaken
with the bellows of their breath, and he touched their new horns.
The little mice of the fields fled about him, and he gave them his
unchanged position, and the night birds murmured above and he
moved not, and the creeping things that he had not numbered or
known, looked at him from a million eyes, and his eyes were there
also, and the things in the trees made walking and running on the
branches, and he spoke not."

Mannered, lapidary, exquisite, decadent—reveling in the Wil-
dean truth that "Art is Art because it is not Nature"—Djuna
Barnes's writing is certainly not everyone's cup of tea. As Field
acutely observes, her art aims more at concealment than representation. She hides more than she tells. Anyone turning to *Nightwood* for a graphic treatment of a lesbian love affair would be
better off with Lisa Alther's *Kinflicks*. *Nightwood* opens with a
lengthy portrait of a character who turns out to be utterly periph-
eral—a tactic designed, Barnes admitted, to distract attention from
the supposedly shocking love story.

The novel's greatest power lies in the monologues by the burned-out Irish doctor who serves as confidant to one of the doomed lovers. The treatment of the "shocking'" affair consists of much talk about the love between Nora Flood and Robin Vote and the impossibility thereof: "To keep her (in Robin there was this tragic longing to be kept, knowing herself astray) Nora knew now there was no way but death. In death Robin would belong to her. Death went with them, together and alone." Jenny Petherbridge, the woman who takes Robin away from Nora, provokes some wonderfully bitchy one-liners. "She was one of the most unimportantly wicked women of her time." "She wanted to be the reason for everything and so was the cause of nothing." "She defied the very meaning of personality in her passion to be a person." "When she fell in love, it was with a perfect fury of accumulated dishonesty." Such epigrams would carry more weight if Jenny had some fictional reality apart from them.

Nightwood concludes with what Field tells us is a scene of bestiality, but were it not for his warning and a certain solemnity in the last two pages one would suspect nothing more than that Robin Vote was roughhousing with a puppy. Barnes's own version in later life was that the dog was terrified to see its mistress behaving irrationally. She was outraged at the idea that she had been trying to depict bestiality. In either case, her prose certainly does conceal more than it reveals.

Field is often illuminating on her style—on its silences, its encrustations, its grotesquerie, its habit of leading you around a corner only to confront you with another corner—and decidedly generous: "What does it matter if we don't quite understand what 'sparkling with the fornications of the mist' means? Or half the other lines of *The Antiphon* for that matter?"

Exploring the connections between Barnes's life and her art, Field is informative but eccentric. Early on he tells us that "the two Barnes stories are the effect of her weak and wild father on the Barnes family and the ill-fated love between Barnes and Thelma Wood." But we do not learn the story of her father and his effect on the family until the fourth of the book's five chapters. (It has been alluded to often enough before to make us wonder if we have missed it.) Field has reached the 1930s in the chronological story of Djuna Barnes when he throws us back to New York State at the turn of the century with this transition: "The mind of Djuna Barnes, no longer held in Paris, could now range back with its former intensity to the farms, Storm King, and Long Island, and the story of her childhood and family." This is not narrative ineptitude. It is experiment, innovation. Why indeed begin a literary biography with the writer's childhood? The novel has moved beyond chronology. Why not biography? But if a biographer aspires to the novelist's freedom he must have a novelist's literary tact. Otherwise the violation of chronology may seem, as I am afraid it does in *Djuna*, arbitrary, willful, and rude to the reader. As a narrative experiment, the chapter-four childhood ranks with moving the letter *E* to the end of the alphabet for surprise.

I suspect that many readers will not realize just how innovative Field's biography is. When in the first chapter, he skims over Djuna Barnes's life in three different ways, they may be put off. When he says, in that first chapter, "One incident in the boisterous months of her residence at the Hotel Jacob found its way into Hemingway's *The Sun Also Rises*," but omits an explanation of what the incident was (he gets to it 100 pages later), many people will simply be irritated. When, in the midst of discussing Djuna Barnes's appreciation of her Irish heritage, Mr. Field addresses his wife—"You'll remember, Meg, how she suddenly startled you by taking you by the chin and moving her face within inches of yours to examine your features with approbation"—many readers will not appreciate the Nabokovian stylization.

One of Field's strengths as a biographer is his ability to get people to talk to him. And they tell him the most remarkable things. Of Barnes's early years in Greenwich Village, for example,

Field writes: "A tall and handsome young European down from Harvard named Putzi Hanfstaengl courted her most intensely. A subsequent lover told me that Putzi once suffered an extremely painful burst blood vessel in his penis while dancing with Djuna." Barnes herself would have been the most useful informant, had she been willing to participate fully in Field's biographical experiment the way Nabokov did. At her best, she was not only witty (to a hyperactive member of the Guggenheim group she said, "You would be marvelous company slightly stunned") she was also bold and inventive in her explorations of reality: in 1914, as a journalist, she submitted to force-feeding in order to write about what the English suffragists were enduring.

But Barnes's biographer claims that by the time he met her she was a querulous and embittered relic, going for months without a conversation, expecting everyone to cheat her, asking Field what the point was of dredging up her family history, asking Mrs. Field how she could stand to be married to a man with a beard. Andrew Field's description of her in old age is, along with David Plante's portrait of Jean Rhys in her eighties, one of the most devastating I know. Some of Barnes's friends, however, dispute it. Frances McCullough says that at least five people came to see her once a week. "They were rewarded with an amazing presence and the legendary Barnes wit. On her ninetieth birthday, days before she died, her little room was jammed with flowers and friends, including a German poet who had flown over especially for the occasion."* So much for friendlessness. It is, says McCullough, one of "zillions" of errors in Field's biography of Barnes, and she claims, further, that both Barnes and Rhys were "victimized" by men who presented themselves in the guise of devoted helpers at a time when the old women were in no position to rebuff them.

Field quotes Barnes as saying, "You have come too late to write

* Letter to the Editor, the *New York Times Book Review*, July 17, 1983, p. 23.

a book about me, Mr. Field." Perhaps she was right, but it seems ill mannered of her biographer to quote her on this. It's as if he's excusing himself for any inadequacies in the book, shifting them onto Barnes. The other side of that coin is Frances McCullough's disturbing suggestion that the biographer may be a victimizer.

ANNE THACKERAY RITCHIE

❖ ❖ ❖

The late Winifred Gérin, who had previously written biographies of Charlotte Brontë, Emily Brontë and Elizabeth Gaskell, in what was to be her last book chose, bravely and rightly, to devote her great skill as a biographer to a lesser writer who was a splendid human being. Although Anne Thackeray wrote eight novels and was famous and successful as a writer in her time, she is now largely unread and is an unlikely candidate for a revaluation. Even her best work—her volumes of memoirs and recollections of famous contemporaries and her biographical introductions to her father's novels—suffers from garrulousness, the sunny expansiveness which made her such a pleasure to know. However, Gérin did not write this book to canonize the work. It is, she says in her preface, "more than time that this highly original, lovable woman should be better known." I think everyone who reads this biography will agree.

Born in 1837, the year Victoria ascended the throne, Anne Thackeray was the elder of the great novelist's two daughters. Their mother went quietly and pathetically mad after the birth of Anny's sister, Minny, and remained in private care, away from the family, for the rest of her long life. Since Thackeray could not divorce his wife and remarry, the girls were destined to remain motherless, and their affectionate, spirited father was consigned to bachelorhood. At first the girls were raised in Paris by their grandparents, but when Anny was nine, Thackeray resolved to make a home for them in London and to live with them himself. They became his chief delight and solace.

❖ *Anne Thackeray Ritchie: A Biography* (New York: Oxford University Press, 1981) by Winifred Gérin.

Thackeray frankly confessed, with a characteristic absence of humbug, that his daughters took the place of his wife and helped to fill the emotional vacuum inside him. He was equally frank about his fears of losing them through marriage, especially Anny, who was cleverer than Minny and closer to her father. "I am brutally happy," Thackeray wrote, "that she is not handsome enough to fall in love with, so that I hope she'll stay by me for many a year yet." His dependence on his daughters and their closeness to him could have been a scenario for domestic disaster, but it was not, largely, I think, because Thackeray made clear that any selfishness in the case was on his part. He wanted to keep his daughters with him for his own pleasure. If they fell in love and married, that was natural and not a perfidious desertion of him. Consequently, they did not want to leave him, and neither married until after his death.

When he died—he was only fifty-three—his friends rallied to help his daughters. Anny went to recover at the Isle of Wight cottage of the photographer Julia Margaret Cameron. Tennyson, wrapped in a large cloak, was waiting for her on the dark night she arrived. Later, Jane Carlyle would take Anny and Minny driving in her carriage. Because the Thackerays knew and were loved by an enormous number of the talented people of nineteenth-century London, Gérin's book provides a privileged look at the private lives of the artistic great. And thanks to Anne Thackeray's memoirs, we have access to some extraordinary occasions, like the dinner party Thackeray gave for Charlotte Brontë to which he invited the most brilliant women he knew (Carlyle came with his wife) but which turned out so dull that the host slipped away to his club before the guest of honor left.

Anny started writing in her teens and made her first appearance in print with a sketch in the *Cornhill* magazine when she was twenty-three. Two years later, her first novel, *The Story of Elizabeth*, was serialized in the *Cornhill* and was a great success, bringing her both fame and a certain amount of fortune. So she was already established as a writer by the time her father died. She would continue to make money by her pen for the rest of her life, but she spent it almost faster than she made it. Gérin hints at imprudence, but Anny was supporting many people besides herself, including her mother. At the age of twenty-nine, when she might reasonably have thought she would never marry, Anny adopted the two baby daughters of a companion who had died in childbirth. One is struck, reading this book, by the flexibility and inventiveness in these Victorian living arrangements, by the impulsive creation of surrogate families, by the abandon with which people seemed to take on responsibilities for other people's lives. One must remind oneself that it depended on big houses, servants, money and a complete absence of alternatives such as a state welfare system.

In her middle age, Anne Thackeray had independence, success in work she loved, and a circle of devoted friends, but she was lonely at the core of her being. She had no one to replace her father as the central love of her life. Her beloved sister, Minny, who had married Leslie Stephen in 1867, died in 1875. This left Anny tied to her sister's gloomy, difficult husband (who by his second wife would be the father of Virginia Woolf) and her mentally deficient daughter, Laura. The consolation Anny found was typically unconventional and shocked almost everyone she knew.

Thirty-nine, she fell in love with and decided to marry her cousin, Richmond Ritchie, twenty-three and just finishing at Cambridge. He was a young man of extraordinary self-possession who never seems to have been bothered by any inequality in the match. Despite Anny's fame, success and age, he thought he could make her happy, and he was right. He entered the India Office and proved an excellent administrator, rising eventually to a knighthood (which made his wife Lady Ritchie) and to the position of Permanent Undersecretary of State for India.

Anne Thackeray's life is worth knowing about if only because she broke so many taboos with so little fuss and so much success.

She married a man sixteen years younger than herself. She gave birth to her first child at the age of forty-one, without the aid of modern medicine. (She would have two children, both healthy.) Marriage and motherhood did not keep her from work: in fact, her work, which had always been dependent on experience, improved after her children were born. Her relationship with her father remained the central fact of her life, and yet it does not seem to have stunted her in any way.

She outlived practically everyone she knew, even her young husband. She lived to see Leslie Stephen's second wife die and to inherit him once again, this time with even more children, including the young Virginia Woolf. (You realize, from Anne Ritchie's perspective, how preternaturally depressive that household must have been.) Then she sat by Leslie's bedside as he died. With her immense vitality, she wished at the age of eighty to be cut up into four young women of twenty. During the First World War, kept awake by German bombers, she could enjoy the beauty of the moonlit sky, such was her unquenchable optimism. Virginia Woolf would write her obituary and call her a writer of genius. She was being partial to a woman she knew well and loved deeply. More accurately, she said of Anne's writing that the string didn't quite unite the pearls, but the pearls were there. She also commemorated her aunt in the portrait of Mrs. Hilbery in *Night and Day*, warm, generous, slightly scatterbrained, devoting her life to the biography of her father, a great Victorian poet.

Henry James said of Anne Thackeray that she combined a minimum of good sense with a maximum of good feeling. It is impossible to read this biography—as it was, apparently, impossible to know her—without loving her. Anne Thackeray may or may not have inherited her father's genius. She certainly inherited his splendid humanity, never more fully suggested than here. One must be grateful to Winifred Gérin for her daring and imaginative choice of a subject. It has produced a work of remarkable sweetness, an intensely moving record of good people, living in good faith, with a great capacity for love and pleasure and no guilt about finding them, even in odd places, in a life sufficiently filled with pain.

ISAK DINESEN

✦ ✦ ✦

Isak Dinesen did not start writing in a serious and sustained way until her life—her life in the body as opposed to the imagination—was over. She was past forty. Her marriage to Swedish baron Bror Blixen had ended in divorce. Her great love affair with English aristocrat Denys Finch Hatton had ended with his death in a plane crash. She had lost the place she cared most about, the coffee farm in Africa where she had spent close to twenty years, and had been forced to return to her native Denmark, which she found inimical to her spirit. Syphilis, contracted from her husband, was affecting her spine—her body would be disintegrating for the rest of her life. The decay of her body —and the consequent closing down of her erotic life—was the price she had to pay for her gifts as a writer. That, at any rate, was how she saw the story of her life, and that is how Judith Thurman has chosen to tell it in this beautifully written, energetically researched, and absorbing biography.

This is, in the words of the subtitle, "the life of a storyteller," but Dinesen in no way set out to make herself a storyteller. She turned to writing only when she had no place else to go, when she was backed into a corner. At the age of forty-one, when it became clear that she was likely to lose her African farm, she played with the idea of running a hotel for blacks in Djibouti or Marseilles. She thought about earning her living as a cook and even apprenticed herself, on a visit home, to a Copenhagen chef. She considered making a marriage of convenience with one of three wealthy Englishmen—none of them her lover. She wrote because she could

✤ *Isak Dinesen: The Life of a Storyteller* (New York: St. Martin's, 1982) by Judith Thurman.

do nothing else and when she had nothing left to lose. Her voice came to her, Thurman says, "only when she had lived enough to make a 'reckoning' with her losses, rather than through continuous exercise of her craft."

Thurman has been greatly influenced by Walter Benjamin's idea that a person has to accept death and forgo life before he or she can become a storyteller. This melodramatic notion actually works rather well for Dinesen—and for various other women writers—if "forgoing life" is understood to mean ceasing to live so as to please men and to secure for oneself a satisfying sexual life. To women who value creativity and who also value a stable, conventional family life, it must be disturbing that none of the great women writers of Dinesen's generation managed to have both. I mean the generation that came to maturity in the 1920s —Virginia Woolf, Willa Cather, Gertrude Stein. The raffish Colette came the closest to "normalcy," and even she suggests (especially in *The Vagabond*) the necessity of sexual sacrifice.

Dinesen was clear about the need for—and the cost of—such a trade-off. "You know that I have said that I would like to be a Catholic priest," she wrote to her brother, "and I still maintain this—and I am not far from being one—but he would have to be more than human if he did not sometimes heave a sigh on seeing the lights lit in the windows and the family circles gathered together." For her, there was to be creativity, but no intimacy. She would give up on life, but she would live in art: "I promised the Devil my soul, and in return he promised me that everything I was going to experience hereafter would be turned into tales." Perhaps Dinesen was making the same point in a different way when she told a feminist gathering that a woman's business, sexually speaking, was "charm," and confessed that if she were a man it would be out of the question for her to fall in love with a woman writer.

Although she was a rebellious young woman, always chafing against her prosperous family and the middle-class morality of her country, it took her more than forty years and that bad case of syphilis to recover fully from the notion that she had to live *through* a man and to relinquish charm (if, indeed, she ever did that). On the intriguing subject of the men in Dinesen's life, Thurman fills in excellently where, in *Out of Africa*, Dinesen is elusive. What was the husband like who brought her to Africa, who made her actually take "the voyage out" that Virginia Woolf only imagined? "Maddeningly without moods." "One of the most durable, congenial, promiscuous, and prodigal creatures who ever lived." Thurman's thumbnail sketches are acute, generous, frequently witty. For Bror Blixen, "conquest in all its forms, though particularly of large mammals, was the central passion." Blixen was Hemingway's model for Wilson, the *macho* hunter-guide in "The Short, Happy Life of Francis Macomber." Dinesen was attracted to his aristocratic prodigality and to his aggressively male enthusiasms. She was not appalled when he gave her the syphilis he had probably contracted from a Masai woman. It was an enlargement of her experience, a spiritual opportunity. (Is that, too, typical of women writers—that pathetic grasping at every piece of bad luck as "experience," an escape from the usual constrictions of women's lives? Dinesen regarded her syphilis much the way Woolf did her insanity.) It was Blixen, finally, who asked for a divorce in order to marry someone else.

Dinesen did not want to divorce him. For her, love and marriage were quite separate things. She wanted to keep intact both her marriage and her relationship with Denys Finch Hatton, who would never have married her. Irresistibly charming, handsome, well educated, the son of the Earl of Winchilsea, a kind of Sebastian Flyte without the dissoluteness, Finch Hatton guarded his independence jealously. He went on safaris. He took frequent trips back to England. He dropped in on "Tania," as Dinesen was known to her friends, when he felt like it, but rarely for a long stretch. Their pleasure together was made keener by the awareness of his impending departure. The threat of loss played a part in even her happiest moments. "Only those who are prepared to die can live freely" was one of the mottoes she lived by. She courted death, welcomed the edge it gave to life. Her erotic highs—whether with Blixen or Finch Hatton—seem to have come on hunting safaris. (She would have scorned photographic safaris as putting nothing at stake.) When a lion threatened her farm, Dinesen resisted her manager's plea to lay a poisoned trap for it. She considered poison ignoble. She and Finch Hatton would face the lion directly—their lives against its life. "Let us go," she said to her lover with the offhand grandeur she so admired, "and risk our entirely worthless lives."

Thurman brings to bear on the story of the growth of Dinesen's identity all the intensity and intelligence one might bring to bear on the story of the growth of a nation. At times this seems faintly ludicrous. The book is draped in reverence. Nevertheless, her treatment is always thoughtful and richly informed, and I suppose if we take the growth of an imaginative life seriously, we must be prepared for a chapter on the significance to Dinesen of her Aunt Bess, and another on the contrast between the temperaments of her mother's family and her father's. The effect of presenting Dinesen's early experiences as so uniformly meaningful, however, is to make the great work of her later years seem somehow inevitable. The late works are continually invoked to dignify earlier traumas, conflicts, adventures. Future and past reify each other.

For example, Dinesen shoots a lion and sees it flayed. She admires its physical structure. It has no fat whatsoever. "That economy," comments Thurman, "was a quality she would strive for in her own works of art, her own figure, and her fate." Not only is this beating a dead lion, but it gives a false sense of the relationship between experience and art. Thurman seems to believe that it is what one has done, what one has lost, what one has accepted that makes one a writer. Isn't there more—more of a strictly literary nature—to it than that? A fuller discussion of the writing Dinesen did when she was still in Africa, and of the actual production of *Seven Gothic Tales, Out of Africa* and *Winter's Tales* when she returned to Denmark, would have given us a greater sense of the specifically literary reality of Dinesen's life.

Americans have always loved Isak Dinesen, and she felt particularly close to her American audience. *Seven Gothic Tales*, her first book, was accepted for publication in the United States before anywhere else and was received more enthusiastically here than in Dinesen's native country. Almost all her books were Book-of-the-Month Club selections, and since Dinesen confused this distinction with literary prizes rewarding merit, it meant a great deal to her. When she finally visited America, in her seventies, close to death, weighing less than eighty-five pounds, bones enclosed in skin and swathed in furs and a turban, her carefully constructed public persona—a mixture of witch, *grande dame* and *memento mori*—went over much better with Americans than it did with Danes, who sometimes found her absurd and affected.

Her appearance at the YMHA Poetry Center in New York in 1959, for which she recited one of her tales completely from memory, was such a sensation that she was asked back for two more appearances. "There was an astonishing current between Dinesen and her audience," writes Thurman. "This was the wise, noble, and heroic survivor of the past—the master—they had been expecting." Seeing Dinesen as she wished to be seen, Americans brought out the best in her. She put so much energy into her American tour that she reached the point of exhaustion (never very far away) and had to be hospitalized. But she was grateful for the reception. As another of her mottoes had it, "To live is not necessary; to navigate is." In Denmark, regarded more skeptically, she was often depressed or unwell. She did not navigate so well in those waters. She merely wrote her best work there.

Because of the particular bond between Dinesen and her American audience, it seems right that an American should have written this most satisfying and intelligently sympathetic portrait of her life. Thurman's sympathy extends to perpetuating the illusion—which Dinesen, an aristocrat by choice if not by birth, would certainly have wanted perpetuated—that her work was the product not of daily effort or hard thought but of her experience and her spirit.

CHRISTINA ROSSETTI

✤ ✤ ✤

This is a brisk and sensible biography of one of English literary history's most enigmatic figures. Perhaps because her brother's life was so flamboyant, Christina Rossetti's own life seems all the more quiet and restrained. On the one hand, poetry, sex and death; on the other, poetry, piety, gentility.

The sensational incidents of Dante Gabriel Rossetti's life are well known. Poet and painter, Victorian London's leading Bohemian artist, the bad boy everyone loved to help, he discovered a great beauty and a talented artist in a milliner's apprentice, Lizzie Siddal, married her when she was virtually on her deathbed, buried his manuscript poems with her after her death from an overdose of laudanum, and, changing his mind, had her body exhumed to rescue the poems for publication. Later he loved Jane Morris, his best friend's wife, and the three of them shared Kelmscott in ambiguous intimacy. Because of his membership in the Pre-Raphaelite Brotherhood—a group of poets and painters dedicated to truth to nature—and because of his friendship and association with William Morris, the glamour that attaches to artists in groups attaches to D. G. Rossetti. Because in his later years he sought oblivion through chloral and whiskey, he has also the glamour we ascribe to self-destructive genius.

Meanwhile, his sister, also a very talented poet, lived at home, cared for their mother, and devoted herself to her art and the Church of England, whose doctrine and ritual were the center of her life. She received two proposals of marriage and turned them both down, ostensibly for religious reasons: the gentlemen were

✤ *Christina Rossetti: A Divided Life* (New York: Rinehart & Winston, 1981) by Georgina Battiscombe.

not believing Anglicans. Christina's religion seems part of a larger fastidiousness, a refusal to immerse herself in the pitch and mire of ordinary life, especially sexual life. If it were not for this fine arrogance in her character, for the mass and quality of her work, and for her fame (in her time American readers thought more highly of her poetry than her brother's), one might be tempted to present her life as an example of what Virginia Woolf called the plight of Shakespeare's sister, the woman of great talent prevented from realizing it because of cultural restrictions on experience and expression. And it is true that Christina was not allowed to join the Pre-Raphaelite Brotherhood because of her sex, despite her brother's fervent arguments that she be allowed the status of an honorary associate so she could read the brotherhood her poems. Christina finally ended the dispute by saying that she wanted no honorary status, no chance to read her poems: it smacked too much of "display" and unchristian self-advertisement. Religious scruples again. How often they came in handy to justify her not having what she couldn't have anyway—or didn't really want.

The author of a biography (among others) of Charlotte M. Yonge, the Victorian novelist who wrote largely for girls and young women, Georgina Battiscombe imagines Christina Rossetti turning herself willfully and consciously from a passionate person into a pious, repressed, self-sacrificing heroine out of Miss Yonge. In her rather too simple psychological scheme, Christina's passionate side derives from her Italian background (her father, Gabriele Rossetti, was a political exile) and her restraint from her mother's English blood (although Frances Polidori was herself the daughter of an Italian exile married to an Englishwoman). This clash between English and Italian blood is the source of the "divided life" of the title, but Battiscombe suggests other and perhaps more valid ways in which Christina's life is divided. Surrounded by emotional melodrama, drug overdoses, ménages à trois, in addition to the usual Victorian run of sickness and death, she lived a life of calm, sweetness, and quiet. Its intensity, not visible from without, comes through in her poetry, which is surprisingly erotic. One of Battiscombe's good insights is that Christina's relationship with God was the great erotic experience of her life. Mortal suitors—James Collinson, Charles Cayley—however lovable and loved by Christina, seemed puny by comparison with the love she could generate wholly from her own imagination.

Thus it is that, although she did not marry and never had a lover, Christina Rossetti wrote some of the most beautiful love poetry in English. Her work is a massive rebuke to those who assume that art depends on lived as opposed to imagined experience, and Battiscombe rightly attacks Lona Mosk Packer's *Christina Rossetti*, a literalist biography which posits a passion for a particular man, William Bell Scott, at the base of all the poetry. The object of Christina's passion was everywhere and nowhere, perpetually present and perpetually absent. Yearning, loss, and separation are her great themes, and she writes of them coolly and quietly, with the brilliance and mystery of running water:

> Remember me when I am gone away,
> Gone far away into the silent land;
> When you can no more hold me by the hand,
> Nor I half turn to go yet turning stay.

Like Emily Dickinson, spinster-poet on the other side of the Atlantic, Christina Rossetti liked to imagine what would happen at the moment of death and after, as though to prove that there was a difference between her minimalist life and death. She was not afraid of death—quite otherwise. It seemed a passageway to a better, brighter, and more vivid world.

That Christina's world is not more vivid to us is, I fear, the fault of Battiscombe's biography, which is meager both on the details of Christina's outer life—the shape, texture, and incidents of daily life in the various Rossetti households—and her inner life, as might be known through a full and sensitive discussion of her poetry. Let me offer as a case in point the author's treatment of

Goblin Market, Christina's strange and haunting narrative poem about two sisters, one of whom eats the forbidden fruit sold by goblin men and is dying in anguish for more, which they will not sell her. Her sister gets the goblin vendors to smear her with fruit and invites the tormented one to lick the remedy off her:

> Hug me, kiss me, suck my
> juices
> Squeezed from goblin fruits
> for you,
> Goblin pulp and goblin dew.
> Eat me, drink me, love me:
> Laura, make much of me;
> For your sake I have braved
> the glen
> And had to do with goblin
> merchant men.

Battiscombe notes that this extraordinary poem is open to many interpretations: it may be a fairy tale; a parable of temptation, sin, and redemption; a sexual fantasy; or a hymn in praise of sisterly devotion. On balance she opts for sisterly devotion, which is brisk and sensible of her but leaves many questions unexplored. If she has little talent for literary criticism, however, she has some for quotation, and if her book is thin, it is readable. It will send one back to Rossetti's poetry.

Christina Rossetti is a poet one turns to when most voices seem too loud, when one yearns for the mysteries of simplicity rather than those of complexity. Her greatest poems seem so clear as to defy analysis. She pared away their surface just as she pared down, subdued, and repressed the outward surface of her life. The passionate intensity was all within, as Battiscombe wisely perceives. But it will take a writer less brisk and sensible than she, more sensitive to imagined experience and how it gets expressed, to satisfy us fully about the quiet life of Christina Rossetti.

HELEN BANNERMAN

✤ ✤ ✤

In 1972 a British group called Teachers Against Racism asked Helen Bannerman's publishers to stop distributing her books on the grounds that *Little Black Sambo* and its successors were damaging and dangerous to a multiracial society. In America, disapproval of *Sambo*, mounting throughout the sixties, focused on the Sambo's chain of restaurants, which employed motifs from the book (tigers, pancakes) while claiming that the name Sambo was an innocuous anagram of the name of the owner, *Sam* Battistone, with that of his partner, Newell *Bohnett*. (One irate columnist said that it was as if Mr. *King* and Mr. *Kelly* were to open a restaurant and call it Kike's Kitchen, meaning no harm.) Written in 1899, *Little Black Sambo* seems likely to disappear from the repertory of children's classics, and anyone who has responded to the story's charm must wish that Helen Bannerman's fantasy skin tone had been green rather than black and that her hero were called "Magwitch" or "Mugwump"—anything but Sambo.

Defending *Sambo*'s author against charges of racism, Elizabeth Hay argues in this fascinating biography that Bannerman's original illustrations present Sambo with respect and must not be confused with grotesquely debased stereotypes of blacks produced by later illustrators. She argues, less tellingly, that a slight amount of caricature in the drawings was inevitable, since Bannerman was an untrained artist, but should not be seen as discriminatory or racist since she also caricatured herself and her husband. Finally, she argues that Bannerman was a good Chris-

✤ *Sambo Sahib: The Story of "Little Black Sambo" and Helen Bannerman* (New York: Barnes & Noble, 1981) by Elizabeth Hay.

tian gentlewoman, a devout member of the Free Church of Scotland, who respected nonwhites, believed blacks and whites would meet in heaven, and would have been horrified to think her work was racist.

Hay confuses intention and effect. I doubt Helen Bannerman intended to be racist, and I, for one, do not even think that the text of *Sambo* presents debasing stereotypes of blacks. Only a strained reading would call Sambo greedy for eating his 169 pancakes or stereotypically gaudy for liking the clothes that his parents have given him. (So do the tigers.) He is a spirited, courageous kid who keeps his cool in the face of danger, and we share his delight when the malevolent tigers turn upon each other and chase around until they dissolve into melted butter. But the fact remains that when Helen Bannerman reached into her imagination to create a fantasy playmate for her daughters, whereas Beatrix Potter in a similar position found bunny rabbits; Kenneth Grahame, cutely human moles and toads; Jean de Brunhoff, elephants; and A. A. Milne, Eeyore and Piglet; she found little black children. Sambo and Mingo were the stuff of fantasy for her because they were exotic, and whether you choose to destroy or to redeem what you perceive as Other, the problem begins with perceiving it as Other. Helen Bannerman's "racism," if we must call it that, was not a case of benighted bigotry but of that earnest Christian determination to help less fortunate peoples which constituted the best and the worst of British imperialism.

She spent most of her adult life in India with her husband, William Bannerman, a Scottish physician in the Indian Medical Service. Theirs was a particularly lively and interesting household, a naturalist's household, unafraid of animal life. Sometimes after dinner they would amuse themselves by skinning various kinds of rats, and when they gave an At Home, Colonel Bannerman would set up snake exhibitions in the rose bushes for the education of their guests. They took delight, too, in the new wonders of technology: electric fans, telephones, automobiles.

They could even be excited about a new way of photographing the leprosy bacillus. One of the pleasures of reading *Sambo Sahib* is simply that of vicarious participation in this happy, enthusiastic household.

When bubonic plague came to India in 1896, Colonel Bannerman was assigned to a new research institute in Bombay devoted successively to discovering a vaccine for plague, producing it, then investigating the causes of the scourge so it could be eradicated. He became the world's leading expert on rats and rat-borne diseases. Rats abounded in the Bannerman house. They ate the family's clothes, the Vinolia soap, and even a pincushion embroidered "Dad."

Against this strange but invigorating background of medical research, Helen brought up her four children. She was an enthusiastic mother, and *Sambo Sahib* is filled with rich and loving detail about life with small children. Hay compares Bannerman at age forty-three in 1905 with her contemporary, Beatrix Potter, who rarely left her South Kensington rooms. Bannerman wrote, rode, gardened, raised children, handled her publishing affairs, confronted snakes, and flourished, whereas Potter suffered from fatigue and depression. Nervous illness, "the scourge of upper-class women in Helen's day," was in many cases brought on by not having enough to do, and Helen Bannerman's life, suggesting that to stay busy is the best way to stay sane, provides a welcome model of talented, productive, and cheerful femininity.

Despite the piety which holds that any attention to a writer's life must be put in service of illuminating his or her work, some writers—the self-chroniclers, those who exercise their talent in recording their own lives—seem better subjects for biography than they have any business being if we judge by the importance of their artistic production alone. After her children, according to Anglo-Indian custom, were sent back to Britain for schooling, Helen Bannerman sent them long illustrated letters. Bound and preserved by the Bannerman family, these marvelous letters chronicle with humor and in novelistic detail daily life in a large, prosperous colonial household at the turn of the century. They are the backbone of Hay's book and provide it with its rich particularity.

Read as literary biography, *Sambo Sahib* is feeble. Occasional speculations about why Bannerman did not turn to writing adult fiction when her children were grown or whether, had she been childless, she would have written more do not seem to the point with this person, this talent. Despite Hay's attempt to mold the fact into significance, it doesn't seem to matter that *Little Black Sambo* was written on a journey to Madras from the hill town of Kodaicanal, where Bannerman had left her daughters, and not, as has been previously thought, after she left them in Edinburgh. How she produced, in her first attempt (none of *Sambo's* successors was as good), a book which is so close to folk tale that it seems unauthored remains, in important ways, a mystery. Nevertheless, *Sambo Sahib* succeeds on different grounds, as a book about the British in India, as a book about an admirable woman.

Hay is not always hard enough on her own prose ("Two things about Helen's approach are clear: she approached other races with a very Christian approach . . . ," etc.), but she is to be thanked for unearthing and shaping this fascinating material. Bannerman's own prose and her acute eye for detail support her biographer. And one responds to the sheer good-heartedness of both subject and biographer. As Hay says, characters like Helen and Will Bannerman, "moulded by generations of Christian example and influence, are less and less common today. Like rare species, they only linger on in remote parts." Consider by what ironies of history this good Scots gentlewoman and the Santa Barbara fast-food entrepreneur are linked together in the annals of racism.

ALMA MAHLER

✤ ✤ ✤

What was Alma's secret? Born Alma Schindler in 1879, the daughter of a Viennese landscape painter, she married first Gustav Mahler, the composer and conductor; then Walter Gropius, the architect and founder of the Bauhaus; then Franz Werfel, author of *The Forty Days of Musa Dagh* and *The Song of Bernadette*, a writer more renowned in the twenties and thirties than now. Her first dalliance was with the artist Gustav Klimt, her last with Johannes Hollnsteiner, a Roman Catholic priest fifteen years her junior, renowned in Vienna for his learning. Oskar Kokoschka was her lover for years. (She said she would marry him if he painted a masterpiece. He painted *The Tempest*, a portrait of himself and Alma lying entwined on a storm-whipped bed, but she never married him.) Throughout her life, interesting and distinguished men seem to have hurled themselves at her. Why? She was pretty, but so are many others who do not attract such an extraordinary chain of extraordinary men. She was sexy —priding herself on her "panerotic" nature and on never wearing underpants. But I think her secret was this: a childhood attack of measles had left her hard of hearing. To compensate, she devoted her entire attention to the man she was talking to. She had stumbled on the secret of social success—convincing the person you are with that you want to be with no one else in the world. She specialized in flattering male egos. Is this a worthwhile specialty? Another question entirely.

She met Mahler in 1901 when she was twenty-two. He was twenty years older. He held the directorship of the Vienna State

✤ *Alma Mahler: Muse to Genius* (Boston: Houghton Mifflin, 1983) by Karen Monson.

Opera, the most prestigious position in the Central European musical world. He had become director only after converting to Christianity, for Cosima Wagner had let it be known that no Jew should hold the coveted post. Conversion or no, Alma Schindler still thought of Mahler as a Jew, and this was one of the reasons she had gone out of her way to avoid him before: not only to avoid what she hated, but to avoid what she was fatally attracted to. An anti-Semite from cradle to grave, she would marry two Jews.

Alma was studying music when she met Mahler. Along with Arnold Schoenberg, she was a student of Alexander von Zemlinsky—he, too, a suitor of Alma's. Alma had composed more than a hundred songs, some instrumental pieces, and the beginning of an opera. She was exceptionally talented at piano improvisation. She took her own music seriously, and, in trying to decide between Mahler and Zemlinsky, she wondered whether Mahler would respect her music as much as Zemlinsky did. Mahler did not long leave her in doubt about this. In one of the most extraordinary letters in the history of courtship, Mahler made it quite clear that there could be only one composer in the family. Alma must become what *he* needed—a wife, not a colleague. "The role of 'composer,' the 'worker's' world, falls to me—yours is that of loving companion and understanding partner!" Alma had to give up her music. And that wasn't all. He demanded that she also give up all "superficiality, all convention, all vanity and delusion." Mahler belonged to the school which regards marriage to a creative man as the highest of women's callings, and he educated the young Alma Schindler in this creed as effectively as Thomas Carlyle did Jane Welsh. "You must give yourself to me *unconditionally*, shape your future life, in every detail, entirely in accordance with my needs and desire nothing in return save my *love*." Adding insult to injury, he told her she was merely a pretty young woman and had achieved nothing in music. Other men had flattered her talent because of her looks. Alma's mother and stepfather, who adored Mahler, were so appalled by this letter that they advised Alma to break off the match. But she—whether led on by idealism, ambition, or masochism—married him anyway.

The ten-year marriage does not seem, from Alma's point of view, to have been very happy. Alma got her husband's disordered finances into shape, ran the household to his punctilious schedule, and produced two daughters. But, especially in the summers when they were isolated in the country and her only occupation was copying the music Gustav wrote (another summer, another symphony!), she felt underemployed and regretted the musical life of her own which she had given up. He told her to read *The Kreutzer Sonata* for her domestic discontent, made love to her only after she was asleep, and, while insisting that the children be present for meals, forbade them to speak.

She met Gropius, four years younger than herself, when she was recuperating from family life at a spa. He was very handsome and correct—so correct he could be bizarre: when Alma returned home, Gropius wrote to Mahler and formally asked for permission to marry her. This request was denied and Gropius banished from the Mahlers' life. Still, it provoked a marital crisis. Mahler could not help but be jealous. He thought his age was the source of his problems with Alma. In his distress, he turned for marital counseling to Sigmund Freud, who assured him he need not worry about his age, which was, seen correctly, his greatest source of strength with his wife. She had loved her father, who died when she was twelve. She wanted Mahler as another father. But not relying entirely on the allure of his age to win Alma back, Mahler began to take an interest in her songs. He now ordered her to compose more as he once had ordered her to cease composing. He wanted to publish some of the songs he scorned at the time of their engagement. Alma obediently extracted the out-of-date but perennially promising material from the trunk in which she kept it.

Mahler died when Alma was thirty-two. Her involvements with

men after that seem increasingly frenetic. Her relationship with Kokoschka was tormented for reasons Karen Monson does not make clear. He was zany, wild, a bit mad. He also understood her very well. A few sentences from Kokoschka's autobiography give more perspective on Alma Mahler than anything Monson writes about her: "It must have been very difficult for her to take leave of the little man [Mahler] on his bier and to find herself suddenly removed from the atmosphere of fame and consequence that she had shared with her husband. What had bound her to Mahler was perhaps not so much a great love as a great passion for music. In the last years of his life there had also been the excitements, intrigues and feuds of a small section of Viennese society, the sort of thing she revelled in all her life." Although Kokoschka was not Jewish, he was too bohemian to be respectable, and she reacted to him as she did to Jews—with a combination of excitement and distaste.

She seems to have gone after Gropius as a cure for her tormented love for Kokoschka. Also, Gropius was impeccably Aryan. Monson implies that Alma married him for that reason and for his looks. She went after him in January 1915. He had been wounded in the war. She tracked him down to a German army hospital and arranged to meet him in Berlin. She was determined to make him want her again, and (wondrous effects of a panerotic nature) she succeeded. But the man she married because of his Aryan credentials seems to have bored her to death. Her erotic nature was perverse: what was publicly acceptable was tedious. Mahler had been inappropriate, and Franz Werfel would be inappropriate, and, for different reasons, Kokoschka. "But it *is* appropriate," she complained during her second marriage, "to vegetate with Walter Gropius in Weimar for the rest of my life."

She had married Gropius in August 1915. By 1917 she was already deeply attracted to Franz Werfel, poet, rebel, Jew. Eventually she would divorce Gropius and marry Werfel. In her diary, she tries futilely to work out which of her many men, living or

dead, is most important to her. One minute it is Oskar, another
Gustav. "Werfel is far from my thoughts, Walter is vague, Fraen-
kel [Mahler's New York physician, another suitor] is lost and
gone, and Oskar is near. Why did I never understand that genius?
We could have turned the world around together." But on another
day: "Now I know suddenly, and with incredible clarity, that I
love Gustav and will love him forever, and that I am always
looking for him, even since his death—but I will not find him.
Everyone who comes near me is immature and negligible—Kokoschka, Werfel, important artists—they're nothing next to him."

Her diaries, as quoted by Monson, are an unrelieved record of
complaint. The great flatterer of male egos seems to have been
perennially discontent. At age fifty-seven, she is still complaining.
"My marriage is not really a marriage anymore. I live unhappily
next to Werfel, whose monologues no longer know any bounds."
They flee the Nazis and wind up in Hollywood, Alma resentful at
the exile, feeling she has been (in Monson's words) "consigned
to wander with the Jews and share a fate that should not have
been hers." One night in 1946, after a performance of Mahler's
Fourth Symphony, she realizes that "she had not really liked
Gustav's music, had not been very interested in Franz's writing,
but had been—and still was—impressed by Oskar's work." She
is sixty-seven, a widow again. She is *still* trying to figure out
which man is important to her. What has all this loving and
marrying taught her? What has it brought her?

Karen Monson avoids discussing the many interesting questions raised by Alma Mahler's life. Is her compulsive romancing
connected with the frustration of her talent? Was there a talent
worth cultivating? If so, at what point did it become too late for
her to return to it? What *really* made her so attractive to all those
men? Why should we care about Alma at all? Relying heavily on
Alma Mahler's diaries, Monson takes too much her subject's confused point of view on her own life. Monson does not stand back
enough to assess the force of Alma Mahler's personality com-

pared to other personalities—the significance of her life as opposed to other lives. This is a sprightly account of a superficially remarkable life which I kept hoping would leave the surface and find some depth. It didn't. It is also clumsily written. Monson is capable of describing a man as a person "of the male persuasion" and of producing sentences like this one: "One of the new difficulties she had to face was the sartorial fastidiousness that had recently befallen her husband."

Alma Mahler achieved the Triple Crown of matrimony: a famous musician, a famous architect, a famous writer. Her life was the *reductio ad absurdum* of one sort of female calling: the attracting, securing, and nurturing of creative men. How many women justify their lives by the men they have married or bedded? How many have as much to boast of as Alma Mahler? But was it enough for her? The testimony of her diaries is "No."

DIANE ARBUS

✤ ✤ ✤

In 1965 three Diane Arbus photographs were included in a show at the Museum of Modern Art: two of New Jersey nudists and one of female impersonators backstage. The photo department's librarian had to come in early each morning to wipe the spit off them. Arbus's images, which outraged and disgusted people when they were first exhibited, have since become classics: a transvestite at "her" birthday party with a box of Kotex in the background, a young man in hair curlers, a Mexican dwarf dressed only in towel and hat, retarded people in Halloween masks cavorting in a meadow, an albino sword swallower, twins, triplets, mismatched lovers, smug nudists with ugly bodies.

Arbus photographed these people close up, head on, without blinking, without condescension. The photographs strongly imply a dialogue between herself and her subjects. It is hard to look at them without wondering what led her to seek out such marginal people and what the nature of her bond with them was. Patricia Bosworth's spirited biography of Arbus suggests that what animates her photographs is envy and an electricity it would be coy not to call sexual.

Arbus was the pampered daughter of a wealthy Jewish retailing family in New York. Her father, David Nemerov, had been a window dresser at Russeks, a thriving fur store; he had married the boss's beautiful daughter, Gertrude. Under Nemerov's stylish guidance, Russeks expanded into a full-line department store and moved to Fifth Avenue in the year of Diane's birth, 1923. Diane, her sister, Renée, and their older brother, Howard Nemerov, the

✤ *Diane Arbus: A Biography* (New York: Knopf, 1984) by Patricia Bosworth.

poet, grew up in a large, dark apartment on Central Park West, he with his nanny, the girls with theirs. Gertrude Nemerov stayed in bed until eleven, smoking, drinking coffee, and chatting on the phone. Eventually she would set out, in chauffeur-driven limousine, for some shopping at the family store.

Diane Arbus suffered from what Bosworth calls "the secret pain of being kept immune." She would remember discovering a shanty town in Central Park during the Depression which she wanted—but was forbidden by her nanny—to explore. Brought up in a household that systematically, and in the name of privilege, kept her from experience, she embarked on a passionate, almost compulsive, search for what she'd been kept from, for a way out of the gilded cage. As a teenager she rode the subways looking for eccentrics and then trailed them home. Reality was what you were not supposed to see. Traveling to Fieldston, her school in the Bronx, she counted thirteen exhibitionists in four years. She always made herself look. Behind her photographs lies a rich kid's sense that deprived and traumatized people are realer than she is.

At eighteen, she married Allan Arbus. (Now an actor, he appeared occasionally as Sidney, the psychiatrist, on M*A*S*H.) It was a storybook marriage for much of the time it lasted (twenty-eight years, two daughters). The two worked together, a successful fashion photography team in the golden age of commercial photography. Television was not yet competing with magazines for advertising money—fortunately for the Arbuses, who got no income from David Nemerov. Russeks, by the 1950s, was not doing so well. Times had changed; furs, the backbone of Russeks' business, were out. It is one of Patricia Bosworth's strengths as a biographer that she notices such things, sketching in trends in social and cultural history unobtrusively but knowledgeably. A biography of Diane Arbus, an obsessive and inward person, might easily have been obsessively psychological. Bosworth avoids this by setting Arbus's life into a vivid context—Manhattan, especially the fashion world, through three decades. She is particularly good at using testimony from Arbus's friends. "I was astonished when she surfaced with all those freak pictures," said one associate from the fashion years. "She was as bland and colorless as we all were back then." Bosworth comments, "Isolated by their loyalties to their marriages, these women never confided that they were secretly a little embarrassed about having careers." All along, Bosworth maintains an ideal focal length, not so close up that it ignores background, not so distant that her gifted and complex object is diminished.

Arbus left fashion photography in 1957 to concentrate on her own art. She took a class at the New School from Lisette Model, best known for her photographs of the "very fat or very thin, very rich or very poor." Model encouraged Arbus to photograph the subjects she was drawn to but had thought of as evil. "Evil or not," Model told her, "if you don't photograph what you are compelled to photograph, then you'll never photograph." Arbus began hanging out at Hubert's Freak Museum on 42nd Street and Broadway. She pursued giants and dwarfs. She haunted the underworld, staying out much of the night. She went into flophouses, brothels, transvestite hotels, bondage houses. Her explorations would have been daring for a man; they were doubly daring for a woman. She appears fearless, but, says Bosworth, "she was *always* frightened, no matter what she did—she lived with fear and overcoming fear every day of her life." Indeed, terror became her remedy for boredom and the depressive strain that seemed to run in her family.

Photographic explorations were allied to sexual explorations. "The more successful she became with her camera, the more aggressive she became sexually; the camera . . . gave her access to forbidden places and she took advantage of that." She wanted to photograph, and go to bed with, as many kinds of people as possible. She considered sex the quickest way of breaking through a person's façade, and breaking through façades in one way or another was the driving passion of her life.

Arbus's great photographs were produced in a period of less than ten years. Suffering from a depression she could not shake, perhaps congenital, perhaps brought on by a lengthy bout of hepatitis, she committed suicide in 1971. Her short working life coincided with a period of great vitality and greater than usual insanity in American life, and in retrospect, her sympathy for the devil seems a quintessential expression of the 1960s. Sympathy for the devil or, perhaps, cheap thrills. In either case, it's the flip side of American rigidity. Arbus's plunge into the dark world will ring some familiar bells—if only in fantasy. "I was born way up the ladder of middle-class respectability and I've been clambering down as fast as I could ever since," she said.

Time and the extent of her own influence have changed the look of her photographs. Their snapshot aesthetic is familiar by now. Her character studies seem less satiric than heroic. There appears to be less of a gap between the offbeat (the young man in curlers) and the straight (a woman with a veil on Fifth Avenue). The crux of Arbus's vision, as her biographer rightly puts it, is "the freakishness in normalcy, the normalcy in freakishness."

FACT AND FICTION
IN BIOGRAPHY

❖ ❖ ❖

Writing sixty years ago about innovation in the novel, Virginia
Woolf noted the courage it took for a novelist to say that "what
interests him is no longer 'this' but 'that.'" She expanded, "For the
moderns 'that,' the point of interest, lies very likely in the dark
places of psychology. At once, therefore, the accent falls a little
differently. . . . The emphasis is laid in such unexpected places
that at first it seems as if there were no emphasis at all; and then,
as the eyes accustom themselves to twilight and discern the shape
of things in a room we see how complete the story is, how pro-
found."* Woolf was showing people how to read the fiction of
Chekhov, as well as her own fiction and that of Joyce and Proust.
She was signaling a shift in the novel's representation of reality,
and I suggest that biography, after sixty years, has come to the
same point and is about to make a similar mimetic shift. Because
of its peculiar relationship to what we call "fact"—it seems to have
an obligation to the empirical world that the novel does not have—
biography is more conservative aesthetically than the novel. In
elements of composition, such as plot, characterization, and point
of view, biography follows where the novel leads. Biography—and
I mean by that the highest reaches of biographic art, self-conscious,
artful biography, composed and not compiled biography—aspires
to the condition of the novel.

Of all ways of readjusting our sense of what is important, choice
of subject is the most palpable. We can agree, I think, that biographies are being written about kinds of people they were not

*"Modern Fiction," in *Collected Essays,* 4 vols. (New York: Harcourt,
Brace & World, 1967), 2: 108–9.

being written about twenty years ago. Women, for example. Women who are not movie stars, who are not Wallis Simpson, who are not Helen Keller or Eleanor Roosevelt. In the past fifteen years we have had biographies of Edith Wharton, George Eliot, and Virginia Woolf. We have had both "standard biographies" and interpretive biographies. Even though these women writers had to wait so much longer than their male contemporaries for biographical attention, there seems now to be a great deal to say about them. Why has it taken so long for women to be the subjects of biographies? Obviously, because they were not important. As Henry James put it in the preface to *The Portrait of a Lady*, "Millions of presumptuous girls, intelligent or not, daily affront their destiny, and what is it open to their destiny to be, at the most, that we should make an ado about it? . . . The novel is of its very nature an ado." A biography is as much or more of an ado. And what does a person have to do or be to merit one?

Until very recently, one thing you had to be—whatever your calling—was successful. You had to be the Great Writer or the Famous Person. In the preface to her inventive biography of Mary Ellen Peacock Meredith, Diane Johnson wrote a kind of manifesto in favor of what she calls, in the title of the book, *Lesser Lives*:

Many people have described the Famous Writer presiding at his dinner table, in a clean neckcloth. He is famous; everybody remembers his remarks. He remembers his own remarks, being a writer, and notes them in his diary. We forget that there were other people at the table—a quiet person, now muffled by time, shadowy, whose heart pounded with love, perhaps, or rage, or fear when our writer shuffled in from his study. . . . A lesser life does not seem lesser to the person who leads one. His life is very real to him; he is not a minor figure in it. He looks out of his eyes at our poet, our chronicled statesman. . . . And he is our real brother.

Now Mary Ellen Peacock Meredith was a bad girl. She did not love her husband, the Famous Writer George Meredith, and she committed adultery with a painter named Henry Wallis, not nearly so famous. Meredith, unable to comprehend this offense, concluded she was mad, and it was with a reputation for insanity that Mary Ellen Peacock made her tangential way into posterity. Diane Johnson's revisionist book shows why Mary Ellen might have wanted to make love with a man who was not her husband and have believed herself justified in doing so; it does not require us to believe she was insane. Telling the story from her point of view inevitably changes the story told. In fact, I would argue that telling her story at all changes the story told. It is customary, says Johnson, to treat Mary Ellen in a paragraph or a page as an episode in the life of her husband or her father. Her life can, of course, be looked upon that way, "but it cannot have seemed that way to her."

Another example of the way in which a brilliant and daring choice of subject inevitably raises a whole new set of concerns is provided by Jean Strouse's *Alice James*. Alice was the sister of Henry and William James, the one known as a novelist, the other as a psychologist. Alice James was known as their sister, and an invalid. Yet she was a witty, talented woman, who left a considerable gift to posterity in the form of her letters and diary, a gift which, up to now, has been considered minor. Alice James herself acknowledged that in conventional terms her life had been a failure. No major work. No husband or children. No glory. Yet she did not quite accept conventional notions of success. In Jamesian terms success consisted in defining one's own uniqueness, and Alice James's uniqueness expressed itself in a mixture of invalidism and private writing. To quote Strouse, "Failure was a bedrock human experience she could claim as her own. An expert at suffering, she could *convert* the waste of her life into something more lasting than private unhappiness." Strouse's account of Alice James's life is virtually a meditation on the theme of failure, which is the lot, after all, of more of us than is the glory of her brothers.

The dream of writing "the lives of the obscure" is as old as biography. Dr. Johnson had it, on the grounds that "there is such an uniformity in the state of man . . . that there is scarcely any possibility for good or ill, but is common to human kind." Virginia Woolf had it, on the grounds of distaste for the powerful. But neither Dr. Johnson nor Virginia Woolf made more than a beginning in this area whose time may have finally come.

One of the most vital and promising branches of biography at present is family biography, which is one way of writing the lives of the obscure. Whose imperfections, whose human inability to live up to an impossible ideal means more to us than our parents'? From Edmund Gosse's *Father and Son* to Geoffrey Wolff's *The Duke of Deception*, parental biography consists in depicting—and in some way accepting—fallibility. Gosse's father was the laughingstock of the Victorian scientific establishment for trying to reconcile fundamentalist Christianity with the new science, which proved, through the fossil record, that life had evolved much more slowly than the Bible claimed. His ingenious idea was that God had planted misleading evidence in the rocks as a test of man's faith. But Edmund Gosse does not mock his father. His implicit point, like that of much family biography, is "He was a man, take him for all in all. We shall not look upon his like again." Because everybody is important at least to their children, family biography cuts across biography's bias in favor of the famous, the successful, the powerful, those whose ideas do not get laughed at and those whose books do get written, as it cuts across the genre's other great bias, the favoring of the individual over the group, so that even *Haywire* by Brooke Hayward, which comes so close to being conventional movie-star biography, seems to me, in its family orientation, exciting and innovative.

Everybody's biography—failed or successful, minor or major—is potentially worth writing. Critics may continue to judge biographies by some notion of the subject's intrinsic importance, but biographers should and will increasingly demand that the *donnée*, the given, the unquestioned premise, which Henry James argued for in the novel, be accorded them, too. It is a reviewer's cliché that a biographer is worthy of his subject, but I believe I have heard the bizarre opposite as well, that the subject was unworthy of his biographer. The subject was, if I recall correctly, neurotic, alcoholic, not a good enough poet, a flop. The biographer was criticized for not having chosen a fitter subject. But for a new generation of biographers it may be precisely such failures, in-sufficiences, self-betrayals, self-erasures that make their subjects intriguing. Good biography depends, among other things, on a catalytic conjunction between subject and biographer. What is in-triguing, what catalyzes the imagination, only the biographer him-self or herself can determine. A personal validation on the part of the biographer is implicit: a "trust me; this will be important."

In starkly political terms, biography is a tool by which the domi-nant society reinforces its values. It has ignored women; it ignores the poor and working class; it ignores the unprivileged; it ignores noncelebrities. Such a formulation is useful only up to a point, be-cause in fact biography ignores almost everyone. As a genre, it is much more elitist than the novel, which has always taken middle-class and middling characters as subjects. We welcome the atten-tion that biography is beginning to pay to women, but the novel has been paying attention to women for well over a century, show-ing a concern with the everyday and unheroic which has nour-ished generations of readers. To choose one of many possible ex-amples, George Eliot's portrait of Dorothea Brooke in *Middle-march* was conceived as a portrait of a Saint Theresa of the Mid-lands, a woman with the passionate, ideal nature of a Saint The-resa, but no chance, because of the pettiness of her circumstances, of matching Saint Theresa's achievement. To write about women it was necessary to write about compromise and failure and to acknowledge that tragedy can be enacted in a bourgeois setting, when an individual's happiness and not kingdoms are at stake. Many of the greatest novels of the nineteenth century—*Madame Bovary, Anna Karenina, Tess of the d'Urbervilles,* and *The Por-trait of a Lady*—are based on that democratic assumption, and even as the novel moves into the modernist period, with *Ulysses* and *Mrs. Dalloway*, it is still in pursuit of that elusive figure of Everyman or Everywoman. But biography is still shaking off assumptions about fit subjects closer to those of classical tragedy, which dealt only with royalty and heroes, although, to satisfy our secular sense of the sacred, it has traditionally added artists and writers. In biography, the bourgeois-democratic revolution is just beginning.

For, of course, what happens when you start writing biographies about the minor and failed is that they don't seem so failed or minor anymore. When you write about the unfamous, they become famous. Fifteen or so years ago, for example, Virginia Woolf was considered by the academic establishment a quirky, secondary author. That she is now major has to do not with any change in her intrinsic worth but with the spate of publications, many inspired by the women's movement, which has been devoted to her in the past years. And now that Woolf is major, she is no longer, alas, minor. As a subject, she has lost her subversive potential. We have gained a major writer but lost a semi-obscure life, which is as it should be. "Tomorrow to fresh woods and pastures new." Biography will find new candidates for obscurity and dominance.

I would like to turn now to another kind of innovation in biography subtler than innovation in subject matter but equally important—formal innovation, new ways of handling chronology, characterization, perspective. Every choice of form makes a statement about the way life is, changes the illusion of reality conveyed by a piece of writing. As much as his or her subject and theme, the ostensible content, an author's handling of formal variables affects what a biography says. It is because of formal innovation that contemporary biography gives the illusion of dealing more successfully and fully with the inner life than biography of the past.

Much more than the novel, which from its beginnings, in *Tris-*

tram Shandy, has rebelled against chronology, biography has tended to begin placidly and obediently at the start of the subject's life, to proceed in an orderly and annual fashion, and to conclude with his death. If one volume concerns The Middle Years, you can be sure there will be others about The Early Years and The Later. In the great age of modernism, novelists like Joyce, Woolf, and Faulkner were fascinated by the distinction between external and internal time, between time measured by clocks and time as perceived by an individual, speeding up or slowing down in response to emotions, looping through past to future as memory and anticipation, those radical processes of the brain, destroyed the present and with it conventional chronology. A novel would seem wittily archaic if it began with its protagonist's birth and pretended to cover the activities of his or her life on an annual basis. But this is what biography generally does. Where novels routinely concentrate on the events of a brief period of time and get access to the past through memory, biography has largely denied itself this flexibility.

Along with conventional chronology goes an archetypical biographical plot: the subject is born, has a childhood full of latent talent; in early adulthood, the subject has troubles, but they are overcome; his talent, like a bulb pushing its stalk up through the ground, inevitably expresses itself. And, like a flower, his talent after a while withers, and the writer dies. Too many literary biographies still have as their guiding metaphor the organic image of the writer as a kind of plant, whose genius has a seed-time, an inevitable flowering, and a blowzy stage of decay. This image, and its correlative assumption that the child is the father of the man, dates back at least as far as Wordsworth. And it has been reinforced by Freudian psychology, which we must also hold responsible for the tedious way that most biographies begin with the least interesting part of a writer's life and seem, in some crucial ways, never to move beyond it.

It is possible to handle things differently. Justin Kaplan's *Walt Whitman* begins at the end of Whitman's life and eases artfully into a treatment of the years preceding *Leaves of Grass*, where a more conventional biography might have begun. Not only is this disruption of the usual pattern of biography refreshing aesthetically, it also seems to produce other formal changes with an impact on the biography's content. Instead of continuity of character, Kaplan emphasizes discontinuity. Whereas most biographies assume constant development and present later work as emerging from earlier, Kaplan insists there is no necessary connection between Walter Whitman, schoolteacher, printer, newspaper editor, idler about town, and hack writer of the 1840s and Walt Whitman, the author of *Leaves of Grass* and self-proclaimed "kosmos" of 1855. In Kaplan's handling of this life, there is nothing inevitable about the flowering of Whitman's genius. Instead there is a dialectic between the mundane and the miraculous—between lazy aimless hours spent riding the ferry between Brooklyn and Manhattan and the writing of the great poem *Crossing Brooklyn Ferry*. For the Freudian narrative, Kaplan substitutes the more dynamic Eriksonian paradigm of development, which presents adult life as a series of crucial adjustments and self-definitions. This Walt Whitman makes himself, unmakes himself, and remakes himself in the course of the years. "In what may have been his ultimate disguise," writes Kaplan, "he declared his belief in the existence of the real Me, the core Walt Whitman who stood apart from the pulling and hauling of events and relationships." Clearly Kaplan does not believe in "the real Me," that undissolved aspirin at the bottom of the cup of life. He believes in the partial, tentative, and temporary creation of selves. It is a more sophisticated handling of character than that usually found in biography, where the emphasis tends to be on the stable and unwavering portions of the ego. What Kaplan achieves is what Woolf called the dissolution of character and regarded as one of the modern novel's distinctive achievements. She was thinking of how character was becoming a fluid stream of consciousness, or a discontinuous series of gestures and structures, but not something that could be described in a paragraph and illustrated in a series of dramatic episodes.

Point of view is another fictional technique whose appearance in biography is recent. When it goes unconsidered, the point of view is usually that of the disciple or worshipper—the biographer, in short, who has a great deal invested in establishing his or her subject's stature. Occasionally the biographer will adopt the point of view of the detractor or deflator, but then, too, something is at stake: the subject must be special to merit taking down a peg or two. But point of view, as any fiction writer knows, can shift from scene to scene, and should, depending on what the author wants to convey.

The opening of Kaplan's life of Whitman is unusual not only for presenting the poet at the age of sixty-five, sleeping under his own roof for the first time in his life, but because it then shifts back suddenly to the situation he has just left, living with his brother, George Washington Whitman, "a blunt, practical man, inspector in a Camden pipe foundry," who does not see much difference between *Leaves of Grass* and *Hiawatha*. He is embarrassed by the impropriety of his brother's poems, by their insistent sexuality. Through the eyes of George and his wife Louisa, we see the poet initially as an exhibitionist, a misfit eccentric, a social embarrassment—an invigorating perspective with which to begin a biography of a man we too predictably defer to and whose genius, if anything, we romanticize.

Often the most radical perspective you can adopt on a person's experience is his or her own. I believe that life is as much a work of fiction—of guiding narrative structures—as novels and poems are. Each of us, influenced perhaps by one ideology or another,

generates our own plot, our own symbolic landscape, a highly individual configuration of significance through which we view our
own experience and which I call a personal mythology. Kaplan
employs his best imaginative effort to delineate the structures of
understanding and belief which Whitman himself imposed on his
experience. A case in point is his handling of Whitman's homo-
sexuality. There is no doubt that Whitman was homosexual, yet
when certain English homosexuals tried to get him to declare himself publicly one of them, Whitman furiously rejected what he
called their "morbid inferences." Does this mean that he had not,
as we would put it, come to terms with his sexuality? Well, he had
come to terms, but they were his terms, not ours. He thought of
his own psychological make-up through the grid provided by
phrenology, one of the ephemeral orthodoxies which filled his
mind and significantly influenced the way he looked at his own
life. And phrenology distinguished, naïvely, we might say, between love of comrades, which it called "adhesiveness," and sexual
love, which it called "amativeness." Thus, when Whitman fell des-
perately in love with Peter Doyle, a trolley operator, and pursued
him with an obsessiveness that appalled even himself, he could describe it in his diary as "diseased disproportionate feverish adhesiveness," and Kaplan does not presume to contradict him. He
refrains from trying to prove conclusively things about Whitman
which Whitman himself didn't know.

If you read Kaplan's biography of Whitman for information
only, you may miss how much in it is new. To the extent that the
way things are said changes what is said, much is new. But we
have all long since learned how to handle complicated points of
view, disrupted chronology, and discontinuous character in novels
and films, so I think we do not appreciate how unusual such sophistication is in biography. In fact, if Kaplan's achievement as a
biographer is understood, his work could help lead biography
away from its stale Freudian and romantic assumptions, the in-

creasingly sterile search for the hidden and unconscious, and towards a more invigorating presentation of the way a person wills himself into being within a vivid arena of time and place.

If artful biography follows, after a considerable time, where the novel leads, we might well ask, why the delay? Why is biography, aesthetically speaking, so conservative? The answer lies in the genre's relationship to what we trustingly call Fact. The antagonism between Fact and Art in biography is sufficiently worked over. Whether we call them history and literature or granite and rainbow, we are all aware that biography has two faces, looks in two directions. Those of us who are fond of the art of biography as opposed to the craft, who may respect compiled biography but are more interested in composed biography, sometimes regard Fact as a kind of sack of stones to be drawn behind us up the hill of literature. At the merely quantitative level, the problem is significant. Leon Edel, no mean rock piler, complained twenty years ago, before cassette recorders and Xerox machines, about "documentary surfeit." More recently, he has confessed to a sinking of the heart whenever he confronts another archive. The biographer of Shakespeare or Milton may yearn for more fact, but there can hardly be a biographer of any person since the middle of the last century who can wish more material available or his or her subject's life longer. I think it no accident that one of the most satisfying literary biographies ever written, Walter Jackson Bate's *John Keats*, has as its subject a writer dead by the age of twenty-six.

But if fact hampers, it also enables. The biographer, carrying a load (or working a lode) of information, cannot be so inventive as the novelist, true. The enabling part is that he *need* not be so inventive. Certain biographers—the ones who might, with a slightly different configuration of talents, have written fiction—turn to biography because they do not have to generate material from imagination. So while we may grumble about fact, we grumble as we would about a friend with a penchant for garrulousness. Fact itself is not the enemy. The enemy is an Anglo-American respect for fact which makes biographers timid and a naïveté about the nature of fact which guarantees that Standard Biographies will go on being written and being respected, if not for their readability (it has gotten quite acceptable to mock them on this score) then for their thoroughness and impartiality.

Standard biographies have been mocked for as long as people have talked about biography. Largely, the issue seems to be weight. Carlyle inveighed against valuing biographies by their heft, and there is a Greek proverb to the effect that a big book is a big pain, although whether a biography was specifically alluded to I do not know. In Strachey's preface to *Eminent Victorians*, the antagonist is Standard Biographies—"those two fat volumes with which it is our custom to commemorate the dead. Who does not know them, with their ill-digested masses of material, their slipshod style, their tone of tedious panegyric, their lamentable lack of selection, of detachment, of design?" Strachey claimed to have learned two lessons from these dreadful books: brevity and impartiality. The revolutionary principle was brevity, for it held up an aesthetic ideal. To aspire to brevity focuses attention on the act of choice in writing, on the leaving out as well as the putting in, on the fact that more is inevitably not said than said. The ideal of brevity forces you to confront the fact that in choosing to include this and not that, you have, at every moment, to invoke the authority of a chosen design, an intent to create such a portrait but not another. But now, I think we would all agree that a fat biography stuffed with facts is no more attractive or innately valuable than a fat person stuffed with Twinkies.

What is puzzling in Strachey's preface is his idealization of impartiality. "It is [the biographer's] business to lay bare the facts of the case, as he understands them. That is what I have aimed at in this book—to lay bare the facts of some cases, as I understand them, dispassionately, impartially and without ulterior intentions." But anyone who has read so much as a paragraph of Strachey's masterpiece knows that what makes it the most delightful example of the biographer's art is precisely its "ulterior intentions," its deliciously wicked absence of impartiality. Of course he does not come right out and say that Thomas Arnold, for example, is a stuffy prig, with a tendency to mistake himself for God and his schoolboys for the Chosen People. This is what he says: "His congregation sat in fixed attention . . . while he expounded the general principles both of his own conduct and that of the Almighty, or indicated the bearing of the incidents of Jewish history in the sixth century B.C. upon the conduct of English schoolboys in 1830." The ironic parallel ("both of his own conduct and that of the Almighty"), a technique learned from Gibbon and Pope, bears the burden of the critique. Now this is witty, elegant, inspired writing, but it is by no means a dispassionate laying down of the facts.

Strachey was willing to admit to an aesthetic design in his work, but not to an intellectual one. This was misleading of him, but I think very English, for the English at their best often pretend they haven't an idea in their heads. This they call objectivity. And so great is the prestige of objectivity in the Anglo-American tradition that even Strachey, Strachey with his French ways, chose to hoist that banner, when what he really practiced, generically speaking, was polemical biography, argumentative biography, biography in the service of idea.

Bloated compendiums of trivial information about famous people are too easy to attack. Why bother? What defines the genre of Standard Biography is not bloat or slipshod craftsmanship but an aspiration to comprehensiveness and impartiality. And what I hold against Standard Biographies is not that they are unreadable—the best of them are highly readable—but that they are not, as they pretend to be, impartial, any more than Strachey was. Let me give two examples which are mong the most elegant and most readable literary biographies of the recent past: Quentin Bell's *Virginia Woolf* and Gordon Haight's *George Eliot*. These are good books by any standards. Both are filled with invaluable information. Yet, full as they are, both inevitably leave things out. That is why this kind of biography, which purports to be so fair and objective, is more deceptive than the most flagrantly partisan biography. Quentin Bell leaves out a treatment of Woolf's writing, which is to say he omits much of her inner life apart from her madness, leaving us with the impression of a sick woman who depended extravagantly on a supportive husband. Gordon Haight does not omit accounts of George Eliot's writing to the extent Bell does, but he rarely speculates about her inner life, favoring the done, the said, the written. This gives all the more emphasis to the one theme he allows himself, his one speculation about George Eliot's emotional life, that she needed someone to lean on, that she was not fitted to stand alone.

Obviously I have not picked these two examples of the partiality of the impartial biography quite at random. Both Bell's biography of Woolf and Haight's of George Eliot are books about women writers by men whose assumptions about women are so deeply assimilated as to have for them the force of truth, self-evident truth. That George Eliot needed someone to lean on is supposed to be a neutral observation. But there is no neutrality. There is only greater or lesser awareness of one's bias. And if you do not appreciate the force of what you're leaving out, you are not fully in command of what you're doing.

If artful biography follows where the novel leads, we could see even further into the future of biography by seeing where the novel is at present. And where is the novel? You could say it is heading towards biography, rushing to embrace fact. In various ways, contemporary novelists are seeking to break out of the box of subjectivity, of concern with perception and private experience, which writers like Woolf and Joyce led fiction into sixty years ago. In various ways contemporary novelists seem to be seeking to regain the amplitude and solidity of the Victorian novel. So, for example, E. L. Doctorow includes in *Ragtime* historical figures—

Emma Goldman, Evelyn Nesbit, J. P. Morgan, and Houdini—who are imagined as involving themselves in the lives of the fictional characters. V. S. Naipaul's novels *Guerrillas* and *A Bend in the River* are both based on nonfiction essays by Naipaul (one on Trinidad, the other on Zaire) which to my mind surpass the novels that follow them in aesthetic intensity. Yet the press rightly welcomes Naipaul's novels, so exotic in locale, so filled with information about the Third World, as Conradian, bringing into the novel a late-Victorian amplitude and concern with history. I would mention, finally, Norman Mailer, who has been aggressively blurring the line between nonfiction writing and fiction for many years.

His novel *The Executioner's Song* tells the life story of Gary Gilmore, the condemned murderer who attracted nationwide attention in 1976 by demanding that his death sentence be enforced. The novel, which is massive—some thousand pages—covers in its vast extent only nine months or so, from the time Gilmore left prison, having spent eighteen of his thirty-five years there, until the time he was executed by a firing squad virtually before the eyes of the world. It is based on hundreds of hours of interviews with Gilmore and his friends, especially his girlfriend, Nicole Baker, and in some ways it is as much the story of these other people—Nicole, Gilmore's cousin Brenda, her shoemaker father Vern Damico, decent, kindly, well-intentioned people of no great means or figure in the world—as it is the story of Gilmore. But for the sheer grunginess of its protagonist, I can think of no American novels to rival *The Executioner's Song* and few films, most of the latter by Martin Scorsese, notably his *Raging Bull*, whose subject, the prizefigher Jake La Motta, is also a kind of test case for humanity, the lowest denominator.

To a culture which draws no clear line between celebrity and success, Gilmore, in becoming a celebrated murderer, became a success. He was rewarded as we reward everyone who separates himself from the mass, whether by accomplishment or iniquity. The rights to his life story are sought. The media pay him attention. His biography is now worth money. This is the grimy fact of American life that Mailer explores in the second half of his novel, whose subject is not just Gilmore's life and crime but Gilmore's fame, and whose villain is the corporate world of publishing and popular journalism, which plunders the warm body, harasses the relatives, and moves on to a new sensation the following week, leaving a trail of money. Mailer is concerned to distinguish between responsible journalism or even art on the one hand and exploitation on the other, and he seems to suggest that what exempts a person from the charge of exploitation is the amount of time—not money—he is willing to invest. Again the revolutionary principle is length. A magazine story about Gary Gilmore, whatever its contents, says nothing new. A thousand-page novel, by its very format, makes a statement about the writer's commitment to his material.

Subtitled "A True-Life Novel," *The Executioner's Song* is so indistinguishable from a biography that the *New York Times* placed it on the fiction best-seller list only with the caveat that the book seemed like nonfiction to the editors. As a novel, it is unsettling. As a biography, the challenge it poses is awesome. Technologically, it is new-age biography, based primarily on tape-recorded interviews rather than on letters and journals. Tape-recorded interviews, transcribed, mount up so quickly they make the collected letters of John Stuart Mill look like a quick read. The sheer mass of information Mailer inherited from Lawrence Schiller, who did the actual research, is terrifying—terrifying, too, its expense and the legal complexities involved. Yet all that information Mailer had to work with, in conjunction of course with his genius, gives the book its density, a narrative texture as complicated and full as in the greatest works of imagination. Shaking my belief that less is more, *The Executioner's Song* made me wonder if a satisfying account of anyone's life could be made out of less material or in briefer space. Massive fact clearly did not hobble Mailer. Indeed, it seems to have liberated him from the oppressive weight of his own personality. With true-life materials, he achieves the kind of intensity—like that of Boswell's *Life of John-son*—biographers achieve only rarely. We have in this biography-novel not just one life, but a group of inter-connected lives—a context, a locale, a way of living, not just a case study of a psychopath.

Gilmore's leap to public attention from the garbage heaps of humanity allowed the precious and fertile conjunction of a great writer with an enormous mass of biographical material about life at the bottom in America. The resulting novel readjusts our expectations about realism, making most other recent American novels (even so strenuously proletarian a novel as Doctorow's *Loon Lake*) seem mandarin.

All good biography, like all good art, depends upon a subversive effect: showing the truth, the beauty, the interest or importance of something which before would have seemed blank space, negative, trivial, something for the mind to skim rather than dwell upon in detail. The shocking effect wears off quickly. We begin, after a decade or so, to see in the Jackson Pollock painting more than the dribblings of a maniac. We begin to see the beauty almost too easily. That dreary salesman, Willy Loman, seems not an outrageous subject for a tragedy on the grand scale, but an inevitable one. The shock of the new becomes the shlock of the familiar. The innovative work becomes the standard against which another great artist must rebel, which explains why the activity of art never ceases and why biography, like the other arts, has a future.

The way people manage to live their lives without prior rehearsal is amazing and insufficiently wondered at. To provide such rehearsals vicariously, to extend one's range of lived experience, is one of literature's important functions, enabling us to live more fully because we have imagined more fully. That is true of biography and it is true of the novel. We may learn from Emma Woodhouse's failure of insight and we may wish we had met her. We may learn from Alice James and regret or rejoice that we never met her. At some level we do not realize that Emma Woodhouse never lived and do not realize that Alice James did. While we are reading about them, the two women have the same ontological status. Both biographer and novelist deal in the selection and arrangement of detail so as to reproduce, for the reader, a certain vision of reality. Both are magicians, manipulators, creating the illusion of life and significance. But the biographer's greater feeling of obligation to some objective standard of reality—the prestige of fact—has tended to inhibit his imaginative intensity.

In the future, novelists seeking to escape from personality will discover, like Mailer, the solace of fact, and biographers will discover the truth of the imagination. The two will not, in fact, come together as seems theoretically possible because most novelists will not discover the solace of fact and most biographers will continue to write standard biographies. But it is always the exceptional case that makes the future worth looking towards.

WORKS

VIRGINIA WOOLF

✤ ✤ ✤

In 1936 Virginia Woolf read the nine volumes of Flaubert's correspondence and found them even better than his novels. Now the publication of her own letters is complete in six volumes, and if they are not "better" than her novels, they must be recognized as a magnificent achievement in themselves—along with the letters of Flaubert and Keats, one of the great literary correspondences of all time.

Readers of Virginia Woolf's novels will recognize in the letters similar qualities of intense lyricism, although there are few studied pieces of description. This is the offhand poetry of everyday life, composed of details of place and time: where she is sitting, what her husband is doing, how the light falls on the marshes of the country or the squares of London, what strange postures the people around them have adopted. "It's a hazy hot day here; Leonard has been clipping his yews; I have been maundering over the downs, and trying to write Congreve, and theres not much village news, save that Louie [their cook] went in a boat yesterday for the first time in her life. How, being a mother at 14, she preserves this innocence of all other adventures I don't know." The weather changes, and Leonard is sometimes out walking the spaniel in the square, sometimes picking apples, sometimes putting his tortoises to bed in the lily pond, but Virginia is almost always reading or writing. Just as the great achievement of her novels is the rendering in fluid prose of the fluid nature of the inner life, the great activity which Virginia Woolf's letters record is the movement of her own mind. "I've just been walking on the marsh: a winter

✤ *The Letters of Virginia Woolf*, volume 6: *1936–41* (New York: Harcourt Brace Jovanovich, 1980) edited by Nigel Nicolson and Joanne Trautmann.

sunset; and I was thinking, what do Kingfishers do in winter, when lo and behold, one shot out under my feet, skimmed the river, and caused me about as much pleasure as an angel . . . no . . . I dont care for angels." More than her novels, more than her diaries, the letters seem to give us direct access to this most mobile of minds, reproducing the geysers of invention which her closest friends treasured in her conversation.

One of the particular interests of this volume is that Woolf's inimitable apparatus for perceiving and evoking is turned upon the experience of living in Britain in wartime. The single most gripping letter (apart from her suicide notes, of course) is one in which she describes for her sister, who was in France at the time, what London was like during the Munich crisis of 1938, when many people expected the city to be blasted out of existence within hours. Yet, even in those extraordinary circumstances, ordinary life went on. A larger than usual crowd gathered at the National Gallery to listen to a lecture on Watteau, and in the London Library, Virginia Woolf tried to read while an old man swept the dust from under her chair and reminded her to get fitted for a gas mask. When war came and the bombing began, the Woolfs moved to their country house in Sussex. "We play bowls, and try to go on with our painting and gardening as if we were sure of living another ten years." She rejoiced to have books to believe in at such a time. She welcomed the "little drudgeries" which took their minds off the war: ordering food, rehearsing a village play. She quoted Montaigne: "Let death find me planting cabbages." On occasional trips to London she saw the city destroyed bit by bit. It was a "very dreary game of hide and seek played by grown ups."

The author of *Three Guineas*, who had portrayed war as the ultimate expression of masculine self-aggrandizement, was peculiarly positioned as an observer of World War II. She resented the notion that it was more "real" than a good work of art. "Why do people think what's unpleasant is therefore real?" With her odd angle of vision, she could be alive even to the beauties of war, like searchlights sweeping the sky over Rodmell for German fighter planes, or the way in which, after a bomb burst the bank of the Ouse, the river spread out over the marshes like a sea. The war was an unexpected shaft of light onto character as well as landscape, creating in her an unwonted admiration for chars, shopkeepers, even politicians, and "the tweed wearing sterling dull women here, with their grim good sense: organizing First Aid, putting out bombs for practise, and jumping out of windows to show us how." Perverse as it would be to read these letters for information, they offer a unique and intimate view of wartime Britain.

The Virginia Woolf letters are as remarkable for what they omit as for what they include. For example, the most devastating event in the years covered by this volume was the death in the Spanish Civil War at the age of twenty-nine of Woolf's nephew Julian Bell. Yet there is no strained effort to describe what Julian's life or his death meant to her or her sister, who was bedridden with grief. There is only a series of cancellations of engagements, accompanied by the sparest record of the facts; there are thanks for condolences and allusions to Vanessa Bell's grief. "You will understand," she writes to one friend after another. She knows what she doesn't have to write about. The grief of a parent at the death of a child needn't be described. Many of life's most momentous happenings needn't be described. What does need creating, in and through words, is the sustaining fabric of daily life, the tissue of small joys which keeps us suspended on this side of the grave, the fabric of affection.

If a friend was sick, Virginia Woolf sent a letter as one might send flowers. Her letters were gifts, each finely calculated to please the recipient. To T. S. Eliot she offered literary allusions and an ever-so-slight professional deference. To Vita Sackville-West she offered flirtatious references to their past passion. To Vanessa, she offered her fullest accounts of her life as well as her enduring love. One of the most poignant passages in this volume is the series of love letters Virginia wrote to her sister after Julian's death, as though to offer some small compensation for the loss of his love. To each correspondent she offered an image of his or her own uniqueness. Of all great letter writers, she is the one from whom one would most like to have received a letter, for she had supremely the gift of mythologizing life for others. For example, this—to Ethel Smyth, the septuagenarian composer who had fallen in love with her: "At the dead of last night . . . I thought of you with a clap of admiration, exercising the puppy, writing the book —thought of you as a little tossing tug boat might think of a majestic sea-going, whitespread, fountain-attended, dolphin-encircled ship—forging on and on. And I whip and tumble in your foam." Ethel Smyth, whose vehement presence appalled her, provoked some of Woolf's most revealing letters (such as the one which mentions how her half-brother stood her on a ledge and explored her private parts when she was six). Perhaps the letters to Ethel were revealing *because* they were used to keep her at a distance. They had to satisfy indirectly Ethel's voracious need to participate in Virginia's life.

The most conspicious absence in the Woolf letters is that of self-involvement, self-analysis, self-revelation. In pointing this out, I don't mean to imply that the letters are shallow, but that they are civilized and energizing, supremely social instruments which never allow a transaction conceived of as a conversation—however one-sided—to degenerate into confessional or therapy session. Her darker thoughts were reserved for her diary. In consequence, the letters are welcoming to a contemporary reader. At least (and despite the welter of private reference), one does not feel an intruder. But, although they conclude as hauntingly as any correspondence has ever concluded, with her suicide notes, they do not present a compelling narrative of Woolf's inner life and offer no emotional context for her final act of despair.

The editors, by patiently identifying unfamiliar names and ex-

plaining opaque situations, are generally helpful. But an absence
of imagination or humor sometimes leads them astray. For example, when Woolf, writing to Mary Hutchinson, refers to Baroness
Budberg as "Bugger," the editors explain that she has misread
"Baroness" as "bugger" in an earlier letter from Hutchinson, when
clearly she is punning on "Budberg." Back in volume 1, when
Virginia Woolf wrote that she had offered her heart to a Venus in
Paris, the editors pointed out that she had never been to Paris
but was perhaps referring to a lady who lived there. She was
referring to the Venus de Milo. These are small matters. Much
more important is the dating of Virginia Woolf's two suicide notes
to her husband, because at issue is whether her suicide was a final
act of discipline and will in the face of returning madness—a
Roman death—or whether it was an Ophelia-like act of disintegra-
tion and letting go. The editors consider the matter in an appendix
but conclude the collection wrongly, I think, with the less coher-
ent of the two suicide notes.

Few people now read the nine volumes of Flaubert's correspondence. Selected editions of Keats's letters are also successful.
And as great as Woolf's letters are, I confess to a fitful resentment
of her publisher for bringing them out first in a form calculated
to be most costly to the reader. Anyone who started out buying
Woolf's letters with volume 1 and lost heart (or fortune), got the
wrong end of the series, for the letters get better and better. Some
day, surely, a selected version of this correspondence will be published, and then it will be possible to see if there lies buried in
this vast expanse a narrative, or the record of a maturing mind
such as one finds in Keats's letters. But even in the novels Woolf
tried to dispense with plot, as untrue to life. And whether or not
six exhaustive volumes is the proper form for them, Virginia
Woolf's letters constitute something like an extended poetic novel.
They are destined to be a radiant addition to our literary heritage.

COLETTE

✤ ✤ ✤

Imagine yourself in full make-up and suddenly wanting to cry. What great writer could tell you how to wipe away the tears without ruining your mascara? What great writer would care? Colette comes uniquely to mind. The heroism of women is a theme that attracts her repeatedly, and she appreciates that trying to look good while suffering is a form of heroism—"the heroism of a doll, but heroism just the same." The limitations on women's lives, which in so much writing by women are sources of irritation, depression, or anger, appear in the works of Colette as exhilarating challenges. This large collection of her stories allows us to share her exhilaration and to sample the pleasures of her prose, even though it may not be the ideal way to encounter Colette's work or get to know it better.

Virginia Woolf said that reading Colette made her feel dowdy, and you can see why. No other woman writer seems to have had as much lived experience to draw upon or as much sexual sophistication. Married young to the successful literary entrepreneur and drama critic Henri Gauthier-Villars, she wrote her first four "Claudine" novels at his direction, and they were published under his pen name, "Willy." In *belle époque* Paris, Colette and Willy were literary celebrities, living hard with marginal respectability, and the young girl from the country had to learn many things fast. Her husband was notoriously unfaithful. When she could take it no longer, she left him and supported herself on the music-hall stage as a pantomime artist, appearing in scandalous

✤ *The Collected Stories of Colette* (New York: Farrar, Straus & Giroux, 1983) edited by Robert Phelps and translated by Matthew Ward, Antonia White, Anne-Marie Callimachi, and others.

undress. This is the period of her life she wrote about in 1911 in *The Vagabond*. In this novel her heroine tries to live independently after being badly hurt by her husband. It is arguably Colette's greatest work and one that speaks pressingly to contemporary women.

During the years of her stage career, Colette was having a love affair with a woman, the ex-Marquise de Belboeuf. Colette and "Missy" spent time together in the country where Missy often—and convincingly—dressed as a man; in Paris they were members of the dazzling lesbian circle around Natalie Barney. (Colette would write about the Parisian sexual underground in *The Pure and the Impure*.) In 1912 she met and married Henri de Jouvenel, editor of *Le Matin*, the leading morning newspaper in Paris. Colette had been writing for the paper and would write more—short weekly pieces of personal journalism, pieces that bulk large in her collected works. Her mother disapproved, both of the journalism ("the death of a novelist") and the new man, although he was more settled, bourgeois, and respectable than Willy had been. At forty, Colette had her first and only child, a daughter named Colette de Jouvenel and always called Bel-Gazou in Colette's writing. Her second marriage ended in 1923; when Colette married a third time, it was to a man almost twenty years younger than herself, Maurice Goudeket. This time the marriage lasted.

The voice of worldly feminine wisdom runs through her stories. She seems to know so much. She knows about "that lightheartedness which comes to a woman when the peril of men has left her," "that bizarre motherliness of women opium smokers," "that groove, like a dried-up river, that hollows the lower eyelid after making love," and "that category of active, rather limited people who easily learn the nouns and adjectives of a foreign language but jib at verbs and their conjugation." She is candid about "the avid curiosity I have always felt for people I run no risk of seeing again," and she is a great enjoyer of life: "I have never turned my nose up at a heated argument between cronies."

In the magnificent story "The Képi," she describes the various stages by which a mild middle-aged woman is transformed by her love affair with a young officer. Two sophisticated Frenchmen comment on the woman's transformation: " 'She fondly supposed that being the 46-year-old mistress of a young man of 25 was a delightful adventure.' 'Whereas it's a profession,' said the other. 'Or rather, a highly skilled sport.' " And Colette, in turn, comments on their sophistication: "I had not yet become inured to the mixture of affected cynicism and literary paradox by which, around 1900, intelligent, bitter, frustrated men maintained their self-esteem."

Women in Colette's work almost always have the last word in this way and in the long run prove stronger than men. *Chéri*, that unforgettable story of the love affair between an aging retired courtesan, Léa, and Chéri, a pampered playboy twenty years her junior, and its sequel, *The Last of Chéri*, make a refreshing contrast to more familiar stories of Parisian courtesans, like *Camille*. For Colette's courtesans don't die of tuberculosis. They guard their jewels and railway shares and, with good humor and a firm hand on the servants, gracefully grow old. Chéri, the pampered young man, does not end so well.

It seems appropriate that the name Colette chose for herself should be simultaneously a patronymic and a woman's first name. Her father was Jules-Joseph Colette. She was born Sidonie-Gabrielle Colette. When she started writing under her own name, she used Colette Willy and only after 1920 signed herself simply "Colette." It seems appropriate that her one name should serve two functions because in many ways Colette blurred boundaries, or, to put it another way, she had the best of two worlds. She was both bourgeois and bohemian. She loved both men and women. She was quintessentially of the country, a Burgundian in accent and in many tastes, yet she was also quintessentially Parisian. She was a performer and a writer. (Once she played Léa in a stage production of *Chéri*.) She is a character in her own stories and the observing narrator at the same time. Her fiction is inseparable from her reporting and from autobiography, and her most congenial length is somewhere between a long short story and a short novel. Her refusal to abide by traditional genres makes *The Collected Stories of Colette* a more dubious undertaking than it might at first appear.

Distinctions between novels, novellas, and short stories do not apply well to Colette's work. In the three-volume French collection of her work, no novel runs over one hundred fifty pages. The Claudine books, *The Vagabond, The Shackle, Chéri,* and *The Last of Chéri,* can each be read easily at one sitting. Nor does the distinction between fiction and nonfiction work well for Colette. A character named Colette turns up often in her stories, as do Bel-Gazou and Colette's mother, Sido. Autobiographical sketches metamorphose into prose lyrics or firm up (like "The Photographer's Wife") into traditional short stories. This is Colette's innovative and distinctive form—an indirect, changing narrative line that allows the author to move in and out of the personal. With a writer who so flagrantly transgressed boundaries in her life and in her art, what sense does it make to single out for attention her "stories," as Robert Phelps has done?

I question, too, his choice of stories. Why, for example, is "Gigi" left out? It is no longer than "The Rainy Moon," which is included. It is certainly not autobiographical. Phelps, who has done so much to introduce Colette to Americans, explains the principles behind his selection confusingly. He says he tried to "include all the stories that are patently fiction yet that have never before appeared in one volume," to include texts that have not been available in English, and to exclude the animal dialogues, purely autobiographical sketches, and reportage. But the categories "patently fiction" and "purely autobiographical" have little meaning applied to Colette. The sketches of backstage life that form a large part of this volume seem pretty patently autobiographical. "The Seamstress," "The Watchman," and "The Hollow Nut" are all pieces taken from Colette's autobiographical volume *My Mother's House*.

Of the one hundred stories in this volume, I count twenty-five that have not previously appeared in English. That may sound like a significant number, but all of them are short, and their cumulative impact is not great. The seven "Dialogues for One Voice" are little caricatures—monologues by a corset maker, a masseuse, a hat saleswoman and others. Seven other "stories" never before in English are early versions of *Chéri*, published in *Le Matin* in 1911–12. In four of these early pieces, the rich young man is ugly and snuffling. His name is Clouk. Colette finds him too repulsive to continue with, so she changes him into the irresistible, beloved Chéri in three snippets that more closely resemble but are still inferior to the novel we know. You would only understand what these fragments are if you had read *Chéri*, and, if you had read *Chéri*, you would find them of historical interest only. They would seem more appropriate in a critical edition of *Chéri* than at the start of this collection of stories.

The rest of the book consists largely of stories that have appeared in English in the volumes *Music-Hall Sidelights*, translated by Anne-Marie Callimachi, *The Tender Shoot*, translated by Antonia White, and *The Other Wife* retranslated for this volume by Matthew Ward. The most satisfying stories—"The Képi," "The Photographer's Wife," "Bella-Vista," "Green Sealing Wax," "The Tender Shoot," "Gribiche"—are all from *The Tender Shoot*, which remains the best collection of Colette's short stories in English. The present collection adds a number of pieces without substantially adding to our sense of Colette's quality. In fact, one is left with an overall impression of sketchiness. Less, in this case, might have been more. Colette at her best is a delicate writer who risks seeming elusive if not downright lightweight. Her fullest and greatest stories are fragile houses of cards—gravity-defying aggregations of portrait, reminiscence, narrative, and opinion. The number of very short pieces—sketches—in this volume contributes unduly to the impression that Colette is a writer of wisps and fragments.

Upon this unwieldy mass of materials of different kinds, Phelps has imposed an order which reveals nothing. The volume is divided into four sections: "Early Stories," "Backstage at the Music Hall," "Varieties of Human Nature," and "Love." The arrangement, that is, begins as chronological then shifts to topical. And what topics! How can you distinguish in any meaningful way between stories about love and stories about the varieties of human nature? And don't the music-hall pieces deal with love and human nature, too? It's as though one divided Shakespeare's *oeuvre* into "Plays about Life," "Plays about Death," "Plays about Denmark," and "Early Plays." I suspect Phelps knows Colette's work so well that the relationship between the stories and their place in her life is clear to him. But for the rest of us a more objective arrangement—by order of composition or of publication or even by length—would have been a help. As it is, Colette's last story, "The Sick Child," a strange piece about luscious delirium in a child about to die, is hidden in the "Varieties of Human Nature." Knowing it was written when Colette was old and sick and anticipating death herself adds to its impact. It would seem to belong at the end. Instead, the volume ends with a fragment called "April," about adolescent love, with characters named Phil and Vinca—which leads one to guess it is an out-take from *Le blé en herbe* (*The Ripening Seed*). But in the absence of footnotes or headnotes or even a date, one cannot know for sure.

Unfortunately, this volume has been arranged with attention neither to utility nor to aesthetic impact. The short pieces Colette wrote for weekly publication in newspapers are presented as equal in weight to her more articulated works of art. Colette deserves better.

JEAN RHYS

✤ ✤ ✤

Jean Rhys died in 1979 at the age of eighty-nine in the midst of "writing" her autobiography. I say "writing" advisedly, because she was too infirm to manage a pen and had to dictate her recollections of her childhood on the Caribbean island of Dominica; her desperate, marginal existence as a young woman in England before the first world war; her precarious married life in Paris in the 1920s. In a sense, the effort was superfluous, since she had already written the story of much of her life in the four short novels published between 1928 and 1939 (*Quartet, After Leaving Mr. Mackenzie, Voyage in the Dark,* and *Good Morning, Midnight*) and, more complexly transformed, in *Wide Sargasso Sea*, published in 1966, after she had been lost to the literary world for twenty years, presumed dead by some and extraordinarily rediscovered—she herself replied to a request for information about her whereabouts—living in Devon with her third husband.

Few good writers have been as unabashedly autobiographical as Jean Rhys, who told a *Paris Review* interviewer, "I guess I write about myself because that's all I really know." Such a confession is distinctly unfashionable. How often are novelists rebuked for writing "thinly veiled autobiography," as though one's life, if used at all as a subject for fiction, should be thickly, opaquely muffled. Aesthetic descendants of Flaubert, Joyce, and James, we expect our writers to be everywhere present in their works in style, but not in material. We demand of them broad understanding, projective imaginations. A knowledge of classes, idioms, and land-

✤ *Smile Please: An Unfinished Autobiography* (New York: Harper & Row, 1980) by Jean Rhys and *The Letters of Jean Rhys* (New York: Viking, 1984) edited by Francis Wyndham and Diana Melly.

scapes other than their own is a mark of greatness (the autobiographical standard is invoked, but in reverse). The old saw telling you to write about what you know is advice for beginners and amateurs only, unless you make sure you know about a great deal, extend your range—like Conrad, go to sea; like Tolstoy, make war; like Mailer, run for office; like Naipaul, travel the globe. In part, this growing expectation that the novel serve a reportorial, exploratory function is healthy, counteracting the potential sterility of the psychological novel, restoring to the genre some of the panoramic vigor of Victorian fiction, but it will tell against the reputations of writers like Rhys, obsessive in their choice of subject, writers with too distinct a commitment to a particular geography or socioeconomic locale. And is it my imagination, or are women, who have tended to stay close to home, more frequently blamed than men for writing "thinly veiled autobiography"? The only greater crime is writing for therapeutic reasons, telling the story of a pain to rid oneself of the pain. Here, too, Rhys confesses (again to the *Paris Review*), without—one suspects—having been read her rights: "When I was excited about life, I didn't want to write at all. . . . You see, there is very little invention in my books. What came first with most of them was the wish to get rid of this awful sadness that weighed me down."

Her heroines may be called Anna Morgan, Julia Martin, Marya Zelli, Sasha Jensen, but they are always Jean Rhys (who was born Ella Gwendolen Rees Williams and took for the first part of her pen name that of her first husband, Jean Lenglet). They are alone in Paris or London. They can't keep jobs, have no regular income, depend upon men for doles. They drink too much. They worry about aging, fuss over their makeup, hair, and clothes. They retreat to shabby rooms, try to mark out for themselves a "safe" circuit of cafés and restaurants, regard the world outside their rooms with suspicion and distrust so extreme that it would seem paranoia were it not so frequently justified by the plot. Their lovers abandon them; their children die; their landladies treat them with contempt. When they leave their doors open, the wrong man shows up. They talk tough, but frequently burst into tears. They are victims, of whom it would be beside the point to say that they are passive, acquiescent in their victimization, for, despite their ability to walk the boulevards of Paris and to buy an occasional hat, they are prisoners, and a novel like *Good Morning, Midnight,* in its claustrophobia, in its dispassionate recording of its protagonist's efforts to keep alive through another day, brings to mind Dostoevsky or Solzhenitsyn more than anything in the French or English tradition. I suspect that readers, particularly women, respond so strongly to Rhys's novels because they express indelibly one aspect of the female condition—the limitation, the dependence, the despair. There is nothing exhilarating about these novels except the art with which they are made, the art which was in fact, in Rhys's life, the only triumphant response to a dreary record of experience.

Rearranged, taken out of the order of their publication, the four early novels record events in Rhys's life from the time she arrived in England at sixteen and soon after left drama school to tour the provinces in a chorus line until some time in the late twenties. At the age of nineteen, while on tour, she met a wealthy Englishman who became her first lover, abandoned her after she had become thoroughly attached to him, and kept her supplied with money through his cousin. She had what she says in *Smile Please* "was then called an illegal operation." This story is told in *Voyage in the Dark,* which was based upon journals written at the time, laid aside for seven years, rewritten, then laid aside again until 1934. There were about ten years (1909–1919) before she was able to leave London for Paris, and the shape of these years, suspended between the end of her affair, with the galling necessity of taking an allowance from her ex-lover, and the blank of the future—that shape, if not the specific events of the period, is the basis of *After Leaving Mr. Mackenzie,* though its heroine is as old as Rhys was when she wrote it (about forty), and it moves from Paris to London, as Rhys did in the process of its composition. Her autobiography is excellent on those dingy years in England before the first world war (all the more dingy in contrast to her colorful Caribbean past), making it believable that she would marry Jean Lenglet, a half-Dutch, half-French poet-journalist-singer of dubious character, simply as a way of escaping from Britain. Their relationship was from the first tenuous, but they had two children, one of whom died in infancy. Rhys describes, in a rare section of *Smile Please* as good as anything in her novels, her attempts to support them by teaching English to French children. She takes one child for a walk in the park, can't find her way back to his home, resorts to a taxi, is so mortified that she resigns on the spot. In an effort to get Lenglet's work published, Rhys succeeded in interesting influential people in her own, resulting in her involvement with Ford Madox Ford and his wife, fictionalized so faithfully in *Quartet* that she had trouble getting the book published in England, for fear of lawsuits. In 1939, long since divorced from Lenglet and remarried to Leslie Tilden Smith, a reader for an English publishing firm, she took a trip alone to Paris and upon her return wrote *Good Morning, Midnight*, in which an aging English woman on a fortnight's trip to Paris recalls her early married years in Paris, including the death of her baby, and confronts her own diminished sexual allure.

I do not mean to imply that these novels slavishly follow the events of Rhys's life, or that they record all there is to tell about that life. She was an artist with a rigorous sense of what the shape of her novel demanded, praised quite correctly by Ford, in his preface to her first volume of stories, for her "singular instinct for form." The kernel for each novel may have come from her own experience, but as it progressed, it generated its own details, as novels do. If one reads her fiction with too easy an assumption of their biographical fidelity, one would conclude from *Quartet*, for example, that Rhys's first husband was sent to jail for robbery, whereas in fact he was imprisoned for the relatively benign crime of illegal entry into France and for currency violations.

It was to correct such facts that Rhys undertook her autobiography. She wanted it known that Jean Lenglet was not a robber. She wanted it known that he was the father of *both* her children—despite rumors that Ford Madox Ford was her daughter's father. She seems, too, to have wanted to correct what she had come to consider an overly romantic portrait of Dominica in *Wide Sargasso Sea*, though the difference is hard to distinguish. You see, she believed in "fact," and in a rather primitive distinction between fact and fiction. Her autobiography was to be a repository of fact.

In pursuit of fact, Rhys demonstrates how *not* to write an autobiography. (That she was very old and frequently soused when she wrote probably contributed, too, to the undermining of the "singular instinct for form.") She seems to assume that if she can remember something accurately, it is therefore significant, producing pathetic, unconnected, insignificant fragments of memory of the sort precious only to the memorialist: the family cook was a good cook; her fish dishes were delicious, but her soup was not; she refused to make puddings, Mother had to make all the sweets. She struggles to remember the other churchgoers on the Sundays of her childhood: there was Miss Jessie, who had been deserted by an Englishman and had ripped up Queen Victoria's picture in revenge; there was Mr. Porter, a vegetarian and socialist; and Mr. Scully, who ate nothing but fruit; and she cannot remember Mrs. Porter. She recalls how, on another childhood day, she botched a piano accompaniment by forgetting to play *da capo*, earning the enmity of the violinist. These scraps of memory, however charming some of them may be, make irritating reading overall unless one accepts that there is no structure or form to give them significance. It is possible, then, to be touched by their very fragmentariness, by the autobiographer's effort to grasp one fact after another, to bring it up to the light of consciousness out of oblivion, by her treating it—however scrappy—like a precious treasure. "I can remember father only in little things. I can remember him walking with me arm in arm up and down the verandah, how pleased I was. He gave me a coral brooch and a silver bracelet." He ate a boiled egg for breakfast. He once said, "Nirvana is not nothingness." All those things her father did. Fragments. One thinks of Pound: "Her mind is our Sargasso Sea."

Smile Please lacks the underlying brilliance of conception which makes *Wide Sargasso Sea* Rhys's masterpiece and, in its insistence upon the contrast between a lush, sensuous childhood in the tropics and a dreary, oppressed maturity in England, more truly her autobiography than the one she calls that. Rhys had the genius to recognize her own transposition from Dominica in the plight of Mr. Rochester's mad West Indian wife in *Jane Eyre*, and *Wide Sargasso Sea* is Bertha Mason's story from her point of view, the story of a Creole beauty married to an Englishman who does not understand her background or temperament, who transports her to England, where she is thought mad and locked away. Readers of *Wide Sargasso Sea* who read the autobiography will be surprised at how much sounds familiar: the Coulibri Estate was based on the mountain estates of Rhys's childhood; the black uprising, which the father foolishly underestimates, for which in turn his wife never forgives him, is based on a race riot in Rhys's childhood and her parents' responses to it; the slave-owning past, the persistent unpopularity of slave-owners, the distant, melancholy mother who makes her daughter feel unloved, the alien and exotic convent school, the close relationship with a favorite aunt—all this is treated fictionally in *Wide Sargasso Sea*, factually in the first part of the autobiography.

For various reasons, one should not put off to old age the writing of one's autobiography. The second part of *Smile Please*, dealing with the years after Rhys left Dominica, takes her up to Paris in the early twenties, with Jean Lenglet, and then ends abruptly.

Even the facts she wanted so much to record are not fully recorded. Ironically, the mysteries of her life—among them, what
she did for those twenty years in which she did not write—are
mysteries still. We learn that she had a daughter who was brought
up apart from her in Holland, but how did she feel about her?
What were her husbands like? We learn that she was married to
Lenglet, divorced, married to Leslie Tilden Smith, and then, after
his death, to his cousin, Max Hamer. From the novels one would
deduce (if such deduction were important) no more than a first
unsuccessful marriage. But which is the real "fact?"—that she was
married three times, or the loneliness that permeates the novels?
And if she was almost continuously married in her adult life, why
does she always portray herself in fiction as alone? The autobiography solves few mysteries about an enigmatic writer, the details
of whose life it would be particularly interesting to know. It is striking that its best-written and most gripping parts, about touring in
the provinces, the breakup of her first affair, and the deadly round
of bed-sitters in London, cover aspects of her life she had already
written about in her novels. What she had not already fixed in her
mind by writing had faded.

The interview in the *Paris Review* (Fall 1979) to which I have
already alluded is followed by a "remembrance" of Rhys by the
American novelist, David Plante,* one of the people who worked
with her on the autobiography. The two pieces form an indispens-
able addition to the autobiography and constitute a disturbing
portrait of the artist in a difficult, indeed pitiful, old age. Highly
edited, like the rest in the excellent "Art of Fiction" series, the interview presents Rhys at her best—honest, dedicated to her craft,
enfeebled but spunky. Plante's piece is entirely another matter, ap-
palling, offering a view of Rhys we do not willingly accept of a
writer we respect. She is drunk. She lurches rather than walks; he

---

* Published as the first chapter of Plante's *Difficult Women: A Memoir of
Three* (New York: Atheneum, 1983). The other two "difficult women" are
Sonia Orwell and Germaine Greer.

has trouble getting her to her room from the lobby of her Kensington hotel. She raves about fascists and liberals, both of whom she equally detests. Writing is shit. England is shit. Life has cheated her. She has never been happy. She falls into the toilet bowl and has to be extricated by Plante. He carries her, weeping, to bed. Later, he helps her with her autobiography, taking dictation. She requires drink to start, drink to continue, soon gets too muddled to go on. He types and edits. She is ungrateful, claims he has stolen her book. Once she had returned to Dominica, but all the clear rivers she had drunk from in youth were polluted. She aspires to die like a great tree falling over. She knows she won't. There are no great people now, no people like trees. "You have to be big. . . . And yet, I'm so small, I'm nothing."

Unfortunately, her autobiography will serve her ill and win her no new readers. Her querulous speaking voice, recorded so unnervingly by Plante, comes through too often. One's reservations about the fiction—that it is narrow, complaining, its heroines tiresomely self-pitying and vain—are reinforced by the autobiography. The thinness of her thought makes itself apparent, particularly in her treatment of racial tensions in the colonial life of her youth, where the great discovery is that blacks resent whites. Here is no complex historical vision. Here is no understanding of the forces at work in societies to produce victims and oppressors. There are simply victims and oppressors. Her breadth is no more than a recognition that the oppressors mean no harm. Her strength is in recording so vividly the point of view of the victims:

I would never be part of anything. I would never really belong anywhere, and I knew it, and all my life would be the same, trying to belong, and failing. Always something would go wrong. I am a stranger and I always will be, and after all I didn't really care. Perhaps it's my fault, I can't really think far enough for that. But I don't like these people, I thought. I don't hate—they hate—but I don't love what they love. I don't want their lights or the presents in gold and silver paper. The star at the top, I don't want that either. And if I did, I couldn't say it, for I don't speak their language and I never will. [*Smile Please*]

Whether she is describing the birds in the London zoo, dim-colored, bewildered, ignoring their food, longing to escape, or whether she is recording her misery when a tacky compact, carried for luck, falls out of her purse in view of smart English friends, the fitful power of her autobiography, as of her novels, comes from her sympathy with the experience of exile and alienation, with reduced circumstance, with the plight of transplanted out-siders, the plight of the girl from the Caribbean, moody and sen-suous, who suffers from England's cold, whom the English think mad and lock in the attic.

There may be some acquired tastes, but Jean Rhys, like oysters, you either like immediately or never, and if you do, it is best to sample her infrequently. The taste is specialized. Overindulged in, she cloys. And then too, depression is as hard to bear in fiction as in life. But read with restraint, her novels form an unforgettable part of one's experience. That she has written a bad autobiography should not matter. She wrote her life into existence in her fiction. Her autobiography has little to add.

Anyone who likes Jean Rhys's novels, will love her letters. The "heroine" of the letters is passive, fragile, helpless, depressed, angry, more than slightly paranoid, and alcoholic—very much like the heroine of the four elegant novels Rhys published between 1928 and 1939 in the first phase of her eccentric literary career. In the letters as in the novels, the Rhys heroine, convinced the world is against her, battles loneliness and despair, and loses. Like the novels, the letters are lyrical riffs on dark themes with occa-sional flashes of gallantry and wit. The difference? The victimized woman of Rhys's novels is just that and no more; in the letters she is also an artist.

The young Jean Rhys was a chorus girl in London, a demimon-daine in 1920s Paris. The story of her life in her twenties and thir-ties as revealed in the autobiographical novels bears a remote resemblance to Colette's. The locales were similar. Rhys, too, lived on the other side of respectability, and she struggled, less successfully than Colette, for independence from men. But the story of Rhys's fifties and sixties, as revealed for the first time in these letters, resembles the life of no other woman writer I know. Most writers build on a success such as Rhys had in the 1930s. Rhys disappeared. She lived obscurely in the country with Leslie Tilden Smith until he died and then with Max Hamer. She allowed herself to be swallowed up in English tackiness. She was poor. She was too numb and hopeless to write. Her "fierce boiling hatred of this dirty mob" (English middle-class Philistines) could not be contained. An upstairs neighbor was rude to her, she slapped him, he charged her with assault, and she spent five days in Holloway Prison. You have to admit, this is a long way from Virginia Woolf.

In 1949 an ad in the *New Statesman and Nation* asked for information about Jean Rhys. It had been placed by Selma Vaz Dias, an actress who had adapted *Good Morning, Midnight* for radio; she needed Rhys's permission to broadcast it. But she assumed that Rhys was dead. Rhys answered the ad herself, reestablishing a kind of contact with the literary world, but people continued, eerily, to think her dead. Her next-door neighbor spread the word that she was a fraud "impersonating a dead writer called Jean Rhys." In 1956 a Miss Smith would inquire about copyrights, again assuming Rhys was dead. "I don't know why Miss Smith & Co thought I was dead," Rhys responded. "It does seem more fitting I know, but life is never neat and tidy. I feel a bit like poor old Rasputin, who was poisoned, stabbed in the front and shot in the back but was still alive kicking and crowing when flung out into the snow."

Nothing went right for Jean Rhys. When her work was finally read on the BBC, there was a power failure in her village and she couldn't hear it. More serious, in 1949 Max Hamer was caught embezzling. He was tried and sent to Maidstone Prison, the second of her husbands to do time. Jean Rhys had watched him head towards his downfall but had not known what to do about it. Max looked like a sensible man of business; she looked like a mad-woman. If she had said something was wrong, no one would have believed her. So she went "all of a doodah" and started to drink. While Max was in prison, she stayed near him in Kent. Their life after that was a succession of moves from one uncomfortable and dreary residence in the country to another. One cottage was so damp that toadstools grew on the kitchen walls. "When slightly tight I can relax—also there are red letter days when I feel that after all I'm as much fun as the next woman really. However this doesn't happen often."

All this reads like a Rhys novel. It is not the only one embedded in *The Letters of Jean Rhys*. Another one focuses on the writing of *Wide Sargasso Sea*, which took almost a decade. Max was sick. She took care of him by day and worked by night—powered by speed and booze. The neighbors thought her a witch. She struggled with self-doubt, yet was fiercely determined to get the book written: "I think I have some reserves of strength. It is only outwardly that I'm a lightweight person." When Max went into the hospital, she had less physical labor to do, but she was oppressed by loneliness and self-pity. She hated Cheriton Fitz Paine, the village fate had brought her to. It was isolated, graceless, intol-erant, and without typists. The lack of typists was a real problem. She wrote drunk, revised sober. The manuscript was messy. She could not pull it all together, could not pull herself together. She had received £25 from the publisher André Deutsch in exchange for an option on the novel, and this meager sum provoked terrible guilt. She apologized continually for not getting on with it more quickly. But this story, unlike most Jean Rhys narratives, has a happy ending. For she did finish *Wide Sargasso Sea*, and it was worth the trouble.

These letters once and for all establish Jean Rhys's seriousness as a writer. Even her most devoted readers may sometimes have wondered whether the novels—so close to her life—were writ-ten or merely exuded. The letters prove the novels were written, shaped, crafted, and did not just ooze from her experience. They also show her to have possessed a moving belief in the importance of the literary enterprise and the insignificance of any one practitioner of it: "I don't believe in the individual Writer so much as in Writing. It uses you and throws you away when you are not useful any longer. . . . Meanwhile there is nothing to do but plod along line by line. Then there's a drink of course which is awfully handy." The most characteristic and endearing of her statements about the dignity of art are followed by some such reference to the glories of whiskey, or execute a Rhysian pirouette into whine—more than a hint that the world should have treated the writer better. ("The writer doesn't matter at all—he is only the instrument. But . . . he must not be smashed. . . . No music if you smash the violin.") Her life seems at times so ghastly, so lacking in minimal comfort and joy, that one wonders what kept her going. The answer is Art. "For I know that to write as well as I can is my truth and why I was born. Though the lord knows I wish I hadn't been!"

Rhys's letters have something of the immediacy and fluidity of Virginia Woolf's. She moves, for example, from a complaint about confusing street signs in Penge to a description of its trees, which "have all been lopped so that they look like badly done poodles. A bit ashamed. It is *terrible* what they do to trees. Why? Can you tell me? I've an idea (another of my ideas) that some men are jealous of trees and love making them look ridiculous." There's an off-balance, scat-singing rhythm to her epistolary prose. Her fear and hatred of the English, her sufferings from the cold, form a bass line that intermingles with happier strains, such as her enjoyment of beauty in many odd forms. Occasionally, she can even muster some humor.

I am writing this after a fierce dispute about a clothes line made of *barbed wire* just outside my sitting room window.
I can't imagine what they hung on it. Coats of mail I suppose. Very useful too.

The horrible thing is gone, but I've made six enemies—at least.
There is also a perfectly terrible bed of old cabbages which I'm trying
to root up. My neighbours detest me because they think I'm putting
on airs.

Some of the best and bravest letters are to her daughter (by her
first husband), Maryvonne Moerman. With her husband and
young daughter, Maryvonne lived for a while in Indonesia, and
Jean Rhys wrote consoling her on her sufferings from heat and complaining about her own sufferings from cold. She advised Maryvonne on how to kill cockroaches by mixing sugar with boracic
powder. (They can't resist the sugar, and the boracic powder gets
them.) Always changing addresses and unable to send nice presents, Rhys felt she made a "not very satisfactory granny" and
mother. Still, she was a mother; she was a granny. Her daughter
evidently cared for her. So did her husbands. And she for them.
We can relax. Life was not quite as grim for Jean Rhys as it was
for the Sasha and Anna and Julia of her early novels.

Rhys's autobiography, *Smile Please*, told us none of that—nothing about her husbands or her daughter or her dedication to her
writing. It did not tell the story of the lost years between the publication of *Good Morning, Midnight* and that of *Wide Sargasso
Sea*. Happily, her letters serve to tell that story, and in a manner
characteristic of Jean Rhys's art, the story is both depressing in
content and exhilarating in its effect.

MARGARET DRABBLE

✤ ✤ ✤

Margaret Drabble, who is in her forties, has produced, on an average, a novel every other year since 1963; *The Middle Ground* is her ninth. She has also written a biography of Arnold Bennett and a short critical study of Wordsworth—among other projects. Her output is immense and varied. She is one of the most interesting novelists in England today, and her career is arguably the most important of all. For she is becoming the chronicler of contemporary Britain, the novelist people will turn to a hundred years from now to find out how things were, the person who will have done for late-twentieth-century London what Dickens did for Victorian London, what Balzac did for Paris.

The heroines of Drabble's early novels were, typically, bright young things just out of the university, discovering sex, marriage, maternity, and adultery (not necessarily in that order) with a captivating combination of insight and wide-eyed astonishment. For example, in *Jerusalem the Golden*, perhaps the best of the five intense and closely focused novels Drabble wrote in the sixties, Clara Maugham, escapee from the North of England, falls in love with a highly cultivated family in London and has an affair with one of the married sons, savoring the complexities of love and friendship within the Denhams' orbit and relishing the distance she has traveled from the bleak family life of her youth.

Drabble's last two novels, *The Realms of Gold* and *The Ice Age* were conspicuously larger, in all senses, than the earlier ones. More sociological than psychological, these novels focus not on single lives put groups of lives counterpointed to produce an im-

✤ *The Middle Ground* (New York: Knopf, 1980) by Margaret Drabble.

pression of the state of England. You can watch the change take place in the middle of *The Realms of Gold*, which begins as a study of one woman, a strong, independent and relentlessly successful archeologist entering middle age, and broadens into a survey of the sources of vitality in a cross section of English society.

The new direction is even more striking in *The Ice Age*, whose protagonist is a man, a real estate developer. Economic conditions play as important a role in this novel as they did in *Little Dorrit*, Dickens's novel about speculation and bankruptcy. Drabble seems to be turning herself from a psychological novelist, reporting on women's discovery of adulthood, into a panoramic novelist, with a much wider scope and more ambitious goals.

The Middle Ground concerns itself generally with the crisis of British urban life and particularly with a crisis in the life of its protagonist, Kate Armstrong, a forty-year-old journalist who has ridden the wave of the women's movement to fame and riches— away from Romley, the seedy outlying area of London in which she grew up, and away from marriage, which she now scorns on principle. After years of manufacturing opinions on an ever-shifting range of fashionable subjects, Kate is tired—of media hype, of the shallowness of her own opinions, of the effort to maintain the sprightliness and good cheer on which her success and identity rest. She is tired even of feminism.

Drabble, with her unfailing insight and intelligence, does a marvelous job of presenting Kate's plight:

> Kate can never decide whether she is a special case and as such of little general relevance, or whether she is on the contrary an almost abnormally normal woman, a typical woman of our time, and as such of little particular interest. . . . At times she feels a sense of womanly solidarity, for the things that have happened to her—marriage, children, love, divorce, illness, aging parents, lost love, rejection—are the things that happen to many, if not most, people. At other times she feels a giddy solitude, and a sense of strength from this solitude. . . . She has

run through what she now recognizes were the expected phases of life, though some of them seemed surprising, not to say miraculous, at the time, and she doesn't know what will happen next, nor how to make it happen, and, being an energetic and active person, she strongly dislikes the feeling of helplessness, the lack of direction, that this uncertainty generates.

But it is typical of the narrative paralysis which besets this novel that this passage of acute psychological characterization is followed by a transition of provoking awkwardness: "Here is an account of Kate's past history, some if not all of which must have led her to wherever she is now." The lengthy account of Kate's history which follows reads like a sketch for an intriguing novel, but it remains a sketch. Cumulatively, the retrospectiveness is numbing. Drabble is too skillful a novelist to have done this unintentionally. She sets off, stylistically, the parts of her novel that have to do with action, the outer life, who did what when, from the thoughts and inner life of her characters. I would suggest that *The Middle Ground* is not a case of artistic fatigue, but of failed experiment.

Like *Mrs. Dalloway*, which it consciously recalls, *The Middle Ground* offers little action in the present, keeps diving off the narrow and perilous brink of the present backwards into the past. The most moving parts of the novel are the Woolfian or Proustian reveries in which the author seems to swim happily inside her characters' consciousness. It's a disappointment that she seems impelled repeatedly to return to the surface clutching an insight, or a fact.

Kate's meditation about her parents illustrates this aspect of the book's strengths and weakness:

The little clever man and the large idle woman, one suffering from paranoia, the other from agoraphobia. One could laugh about it now, but it hadn't been like that at all. She had learned to laugh, to admire, to forgive. Yet what had laughter, admiration, or sympathy to do with the tangled roots in her heart? For she had loved those two terrible people, in the dawn of time, in the dark before dawn, in the underground she had loved them. And nothing in her conscious self, in her daylight self, had been able to love. Was this the problem, was this the fault, was it for this that she sat here, was it for this that Ted had left her for a woman in Cambridge . . . ? Those two selves, that prattling chattering journalist in Kentish Town, with her smart views and expensive boots and trendy house (those boots with rotten heels had cost her £80 at Liberty's, she must be mad), and the child in its skimpy dress, lonely, cast out, cut off—what had they in common? No blood flowed from one to the other, the cord was cut, she withered and grew dry.

The fine lyrical description hardly needs the neo-Freudian point given it at the end, or the price of boots at Liberty's. There seems to be ill-judged tribute here both to Woolf (one of Mrs. Dalloway's most lyrical passages is interrupted by the doorbell) and to Proust, for Kate's meditation is inspired by an open sewer, which reminds her of her sanitation-worker father and is a far cry, as she reflects, from Proust's madeleine.

If you are able to separate the content of a novel from its form, you will find *The Middle Ground* fascinating. If, aesthetically, it hurts the novel that it is so mercilessly topical, the topics are in themselves engrossing. Is feminism a good cause whose time has passed? Should women aspire to unattractive jobs simply because they've been excluded from them traditionally? Is life different for men and women? Is life in the cities really getting more unsafe? At one dinner party, three sets of people simultaneously discuss feminism, the Holocaust and the role of Islam in the development of the Middle East, all surely worthy subjects. And Drabble's formulations are frequently inspired: for example, "the new matriarchy" (of which Kate is a prime example), women who have sloughed off their husbands as superfluous, preferring to run the show and raise their children by themselves. Read as an essay-novel, a kind of superior reporting, *The Middle Ground* is consistently provocative and absorbing.

Through the static of fact and opinion, through the luncheon and dinner party chatter, behind the characters' anxieties and implied by their self-questioning, an imposing entity takes shape: contemporary Britain—Britain of the National Health, the BBC, the Municipal Workers' Associations; of Indian and Pakistani immigrants, new but decaying housing projects, working mothers and child minders; of simultaneous inflation and recession, illicit sex at public-interest conferences, teenagers who crew-cut their hair and dye it green; of advertising which degrades women, and women who protest the degradation; of pervasive ill will and frustration in urban life and "the terror we each now feel when walking down a concrete underpass, when we fumble for a key on our own doorstep with the sound of footsteps behind us." It is Britain afflicted by the "diseases of affluence" into relinquishing some of its starchy character, adopting America's throw-away culture without American energy or panache, a fading Britain, in which acting is the last activity done better locally than anywhere else. Vast and unglamorous, Drabble's Britain is her most important character.

At the core of the novel is the question: Is progress possible? Or do improved social conditions merely clothe, in a trivial way, the ancient sequence of emotional states which constitutes the inner life? Put another way, has the heroic age passed, or have "we," Drabble's protagonists and the generation of readers which identifies with them, passed our heroic age? Between the possible answers to this crucial question—between Freud and Marx, Woolf and Bennett, psychology and sociology, between an allegiance to inner and outer reality—*The Middle Ground* hangs, not so much balanced as immobilized, the vital synthesis of Drabble's previous two novels momentarily gone.

Drabble could have continued to write sensitive, perfectly crafted novels about women, but her career, in retrospect, would have been minor. There is nothing minor about the burden she has shouldered instead: welfare-state Britain. If *The Middle*

Ground represents a faltering step in her development, her widen-ing scope should still be appreciated, her courage applauded. In a career like Drabble's, which depends on steady production and growth and a deepening understanding of the world within and without, an occasional lapse of artistry means even less than usual.

EMILY EDEN

❖ ❖ ❖

The only thing more gratifying to find than a good book is a good book that has been neglected. *The Semi-Attached Couple,* written in 1829, published in 1860, popular for years, then largely forgotten, is a comic gem about how difficult it can be to get used to being married, even if you are young and beautiful and your husband is rich and titled. Along with Emily Eden's only other novel, *The Semi-Detached House* (some readers will find this one even more delightful), it has now been reissued in paperback in the Virago Modern Classics series, which seems to specialize in buried treasure.

Emily Eden wrote in frank admiration of Jane Austen, so similarities between her work and Austen's should not be surprising. Eden picks up just after an Austen novel would end, with the splendid match—in this case between the lovely Helen Beaufort and that most eligible bachelor, Lord Teviot. It is a story of misunderstandings and cross-purposes intensified rather than dispelled by marriage, a tale of pride and reticence. Teviot, madly in love with his wife, resents her attachment to her family, and any sign of high spirits in her not directly caused by himself. She reads his furious jealousy as disapproval; unused to passion, an innocent, scared of him, she loses her vivacity. He is all the more convinced that she does not love him. It is a sophisticated psychological drama played out in pleasant country houses, at dinners, on visits, through letters, in witty dialogue and with clever commentary.

The first sentence of the book, which presents the ill-natured

❖ *"The Semi-Attached Couple" and "The Semi-Detached House"* (New York: Dial, 1982) by Emily Eden.

Mrs. Douglas speaking in a "tone of triumphant sourness," signals us that Eden writes in that epigrammatic tradition of wit and precision which stretches back through Austen to the eighteenth century and surfaces occasionally later in the work of such twentieth-century writers as Nancy Mitford and E. F. Benson. Eden continues, "People may go on talking for ever of the jealousies of pretty women; but for real genuine, hard-working envy there is nothing like an ugly woman with a taste for admiration. Her mortified vanity curdles into malevolence; and she calumniates where she cannot rival."

Like Jane Austen, Emily Eden is particularly shrewd with emotional dynamics, pithy psychological characterization, and the application of the general to the particular: "If a stone is thrown into our garden, is it not sure to knock off the head of our most valuable tulip? If a cup of coffee is to be spilled, does it not make a point of falling on our richest brocade gown? . . . All these are well-known facts, and, by parity of reason, was it to be expected that anyone, so formed as Helen was to enjoy as well as to impart happiness, should escape the trials that ought to have fallen on the peevish and the disappointed?"

A bland, uninteresting gentleman has "what artists would call a good deal of neutral tint in his composition." According to the shrewish Mrs. Douglas, the Beauforts "all laugh as if they thought they had good teeth." A bored and languid young man campaigns for office with an energy which astonishes his family, who do not understand that "a contested election is perhaps one of the finest remedies that can be applied to a confirmed languor, either of mind or body." If Eden learned much from Jane Austen, that cool and confident allusion to politics suggests ways in which Emily Eden's novels are uniquely her own, products of her special experience and vision.

The Edens were a powerful and well-connected family; Emily Eden observed a broader cut of life, at a higher social level, than Jane Austen. If you open her selected letters—and I recommend them (they were published in 1919 by Violet Dickinson, an Eden descendant and the friend and mentor of Virginia Woolf)—you sense immediately her social authority. After Annabella Milbanke announced her engagement to Lord Byron, Emily relayed the news to her eldest sister: "She does not seem to be acting with her usual good sense is Mama's opinion as by all accounts Lord Byron is not likely to make any woman very happy." Emily was seventeen. Her sister, Countess of Buckinghamshire by her second marriage, was thirty-seven. William Pitt had been deeply in love with Emily's sister, but a marriage could not be arranged. This was the high-stakes marriage market. The Eden women seem to have understood the risks, appreciated the rewards, and enjoyed playing the game.

The men enthusiastically involved themselves in politics and public service. Emily Eden's father, the first Lord Auckland, served as Chief Secretary in Ireland and as British Ambassador to France, Spain, and Holland. Wherever he went, his wife went with him; the Eden women involved themselves in the public activities of the Eden men.

Lady Auckland gave birth to a child in each of the countries to which her husband was posted (she had fourteen in all), and for a while her cheerful nursery made domestic life fashionable even at the Court of Versailles. When George, Emily's brother, went to India as Governor-General in 1835, Emily and her sister Fanny went with him, running his household and sharing his life. It was an arrangement that had many of the advantages of marriage—status and social access—without its sexual and maternal responsibilities. When they returned to England in 1842, Emily continued to act as hostess for her brother and to share his political life. She was devastated when he died in 1849.

The combination of public engagements and domestic satisfaction which distinguished Emily Eden's family life informs her fiction as well, giving it a genial worldliness quite different from the dominant spirit of Jane Austen's tenser depth charges. Eden's

Semi-novels result from that tradition of moral commentary, character assessment and sheer narrative that is embodied in gossip about other people's marriages; they have the pleasant accents of good conversation—and some of its unpleasant accents, too.

The Semi-Detached House, Emily Eden's other novel, concerns the unlikely conjunction of two families of different class backgrounds. Lady Chester, a charming young woman about to have a baby, cannot accompany her husband abroad on a government mission because of her pregnancy. He leaves her in a semi-detached house whose other half is occupied by a solidly middle-class family, the wife and daughters of a sea captain. The Chesters and Hopkinsons turn out to have more in common than the roof over their heads—above all, kindliness and an instinctive gentility. Their mutual liking is heightened by the intrusion into their lives of the *arriviste* Baron and Baroness Sampson, who are Jewish. It is *The Merchant of Venice* in English country dress. And along with the genial worldliness comes a blithe, aristocratic anti-Semitism which just might, depending on your mood, ruin all the fun.

Emily Eden is not Jane Austen but she is a fine writer whose life, letters, and novels deserve attention and will delight those who give it. Some sad law of literary gravity sent Eden's work into relative obscurity. Fortunately, the Virago Modern Classics series exists to unearth and display work like this—nineteenth- and twentieth-century books by and about women. The Virago Press, a feminist publishing house in London which started the series, merits thanks for bringing something new, fresh and rewarding into our literary life—by having another look at the past.

MILES FRANKLIN

❖ ❖ ❖

My Brilliant Career is having a second life for various reasons, of which intrinsic excellence is not one. Originally published in 1901, kept out of print for sixty-five years at the author's request, it was republished in her native Australia twelve years after her death and then made into a film by Gillian Armstrong. Reprinted in England, it has come to America with a still from the film on the dust jacket and an introduction touting its relevance to women.

Since Miles Franklin was sixteen when she wrote it, it's not surprising that *My Brilliant Career* should be hard-core adolescent fantasy. The ugly-duckling heroine, Sybylla Melvyn, longs for a life of art but is trapped in the Australian outback, minding cows and enduring discussions of the price of crops. Being a woman is tough for Sybylla, but being an ugly one is tougher yet. By way of consolation, she reminds herself that she can feel more in a day than her pretty younger sister could feel in a lifetime. She will also have the consolation of attracting the most desirable man in the neighborhood and of turning him down, for the sake of her brilliant career.

The novel uses dialogue like "Unhand me, Sir!" and "How dare you have the incomparable impertinence to mention my name in conjunction with that of your boor of a son." It combines linguistic surprise and inertness in a way possible only to genius—or to someone not in command of the language: "In four or five years he had again reached loggerheads." "A change of the team of five horses was effected." Its attitudes are as stilted as the dialogue. For philosophy, the teen-age author offers a watered-down By-

❖ *My Brilliant Career* (New York: St. Martin's Press, 1980) by Miles Franklin.

ronic romanticism ("After all, what is there in vain ambition?").
Of her ideology, which is integrated with the subtlety of a TV
commercial, Sybylla's concluding address to Australian women
may suggest the style: "Bravely you jog along with the rope of
class distinction drawing closer, closer, tighter, tighter around
you. . . . I see it and know it, but I cannot help you. . . . I am only
an unnecessary, little, bush commoner, I am only a—woman!"

Should it really be the hope of feminists that this inadvertently
funny novel be taken as a serious portrait of the female plight?
Perhaps it will appeal to young women vibrant with discontent
whose circumstances are unequal to the demands of their imaginations. But should it? I, for one, do not think Sybylla's mixture
of self-satisfaction and frustrated vanity, of petulant idealism and
perpetual complaint, should be valued as political insight. Nor
should we go accepting the silly idea that we have to choose between our emotional lives and our brilliant careers.

Australians have always known that the book is best read by
adults as regional naturalism—although its references to tucker
bags, jackeroos, boiling billies, and stringy bark trees will try the
resources of a vocabulary acquired from "Waltzing Matilda." Its
most successful section describes Sybylla's stint as governess with
the slovenly but good-natured M'Swats: a lively, hilarious caricature of the meagerness of Australian bush life. At such moments,
My Brilliant Career has a vitality that transcends the comic ineptitude of its prose.

Unlike Sybylla in the film, Miles Franklin did not send her
autobiographical manuscript directly from the outback to the
publishing firm of Blackwood, in Edinburgh. After three Australian publishers rejected it, she gave it to the writer Henry
Lawson, who admired the book's local authenticity and took it
with him on his next trip to England. Lawson gave it to Blackwood, his own publisher. (In later life, asked what advice he
would give young Australian writers, Lawson said they should
get themselves to England or America by any means, or else study

anatomy, buy a gun, and shoot themselves in the head.) The novel appeared when Miles Franklin was twenty-one, and it was a great critical and popular success in Australia. The author became famous in the way she had dreamed about in the bush.

From this point on, the story of her life is like a fairy tale in which the princess gets what she wished for only to find it transformed into a curse. To her horror, people assumed that the novel was totally autobiographical, in detail as well as outline— that the louts of Possum Gully were the louts of her home region, that her father was a drunken incompetent, that the swinish M'Swats and the romantic Harold Beecham really existed. She had expected literary success to bring her love and applause; instead, in her neighborhood and within her beloved family, the book inspired only outrage. It went through several editions, but Miles Franklin felt like a woman who had had a baby out of wedlock: her joy in the baby was undercut by her sense of disgrace. She wanted to forget *My Brilliant Career*, to blot it out. Later, she would refer to it contemptuously as a girl's book, tossed off in a matter of weeks (ten), written out of "inexperience and consuming longing." In this spirit, she prohibited its republication until at least ten years after her death.

In 1902 Miles Franklin moved to Sydney, where she wrote for the *Bulletin*, a nationalist weekly, and undertook domestic work to get experience. As a "corrective" to her first book, she wrote *My Career Goes Bung*, in which Sybylla—herself suddenly beautiful and her father respectable—discovers the hollowness of fame in Sydney and returns to the good old folks of Possum Gully. But no one would publish *My Career Goes Bung*, and it remained in manuscript until 1946.

By the time she was twenty-six, she felt washed up as a writer and fed up with Australia. She went to America in 1905 to study music but discovered it was too late to train her talent properly. She got caught up in reform work instead. She helped Alice Henry, the Australian feminist and labor leader, to organize the

Women's Trade Union League, managed its national office in Chicago for ten years, and edited its magazine, *Life and Labor*. At the start of the first world war, she moved to England, where she would live for twenty years, working as a nurse—in slum nurseries, and, for a time, on Balkan battlefields—and then as political secretary of the National Housing Council in Bloomsbury.

A novel she had written before leaving Australia, *Some Everyday Folk and Dawn*, was published by Blackwood in 1909. After that, her career as a writer went underground.

Between 1925 and 1931 she worked on an ambitious series of novels, a saga of Australian pioneering life from the mid-nineteenth century to the present. The first was published in 1928, but the author was listed as "Brent of Bin Bin." Although hisories of Australian literature note the astonishing similarities of style and theme between the works of Miles Franklin and those of Brent of Bin Bin, Franklin never in her lifetime publicly acknowledged being Brent. This may be an extraordinary case of ambivalence about fame, but it should also be said that she was, in general, a strange and secretive person: when she answered the telephone she would pretend to be someone else, promising to go and fetch Miles Franklin.

On paper, her career seems a full one. She published five novels as Miles Franklin and six as Brent of Bin Bin, in addition to a biography, a couple of light novels, a collection of essays, and an autobiography. After her return to Australia in 1933, she became an active and respected member of the Fellowship of Australian Writers and lectured at the University of Western Australia. But she was bitter and unhappy, whether abroad or in urban Australia, homesick for the bush. The direct line of her imagination went back to the places of her childhood and the pioneering life of her ancestors. By the mid-1930s she had done as much with that material as she could—in the Brent novels and in *All That Swagger* (1936)—and although she lived for nearly twenty more years, she wrote little further of value. She achieved celebrity, but she was never other than a mediocre writer. She was too loquacious and imprecise. Perhaps she knew that but still she chose to rail against publishers and the absence of encouragement for writers, blaming outer rather than inner circumstance in a characteristically political way.

The conflict in Miles Franklin's life was not between her career and the love of a man. In fact, she didn't care much for men. The real conflict was between politically inspired practical philanthropy, to which she devoted so much of her life, and art. To me, her most poignant gesture was one in which she finally reconciled those impulses: in her last years she saved her money and in her will established an annual award for the best novel about Australian life, the Miles Franklin Award.

CYNTHIA OZICK
and
JOYCE CAROL OATES

✤ ✤ ✤

Cynthia Ozick and Joyce Carol Oates have nothing in common but the *O* with which both their last names begin. That both are women and that both are primarily fiction writers who present us now with collections of essays are accidents of no more significance than their shared *O*. Ozick writes slowly, carefully, with respect for the conscious activity of art. Oates is a gusher, with a closet belief that every word welling up from the sacred unconscious must be precious. How else explain her inability to edit herself? In *Art & Ardor*, Ozick's perfectionist, self-critical habits produce a book which surprises and delights on every line, a model—except that her prose is inimitable—of the play of mind over matters of life and literature. For Oates's *The Profane Art* there is not much excuse, except that her reviews—in which she is presumably working under a word limit—are good.

A collection of previously published essays is like a dinner of leftovers. It may be delicious, but it should be served up with a certain modesty. Oates, to justify her book, invokes Plato, the myth of Medusa, Nietzsche, Northrop Frye, Matthew Arnold, and W.H. Auden's distinction between the sacred (whose value lies in what it is) and the profane (whose value lies in what it does). Criticism is the "profane art" of the title, and it is justified by its service to the sacred. Art itself. All the drum rolling seems

✚ *The Profane Art: Essays and Reviews* (New York: Dutton, 1983) by Joyce Carol Oates, and *Art and Ardor: Essays* (New York: Knopf, 1983) by Cynthia Ozick.

increasingly silly as one makes one's way through the essays it heralds: a patched-together piece on cities in American literature, an essay pointing out that images of women in modernist writers are not at all innovative, a discussion of *Wuthering Heights* which contains nothing unfamiliar to academic readers, and a bland little essay on Lewis Carroll. Is it for this one needed to be reminded of Medusa's head, so terrifying it could not be confronted directly but only reflected in Perseus's shield? What hideous Medusa is reflected in the shield of Lewis Carroll?

But the principle of such writing is that nuggets exist—though the reader must find them. And so one reads on. Now it is Oates on Updike. "His world, like [Flannery] O'Connor's is 'incarnational' . . . perhaps because, in Updike, such a synthesis of fidelity and inventiveness allows an escape of sorts from the tyrannical, unimaginative cosmology of Calvinism." Rarely descending from the abstract, Oates is a master of the unilluminating quotation and the superfluous comparison. "O'Connor's interest was in love of a distinctly spiritual nature, but Updike speaks with Alexander Blok, surely, in saying, "We love the flesh: its taste, its tones/Its charnel odor, breathed through Death's jaws.'"

Her prose reads like that of a bright, hard-working undergraduate, and most of her essays achieve that peculiar undergraduate mixture of demure self-effacement—abstinence from the personal—with gigantism, the taking on of everything at once. "A writer who shares Updike's extreme interest in the visual world as well as his obsession with language is Joseph Conrad who, significantly, could imagine the ideal and the real only as hopelessly separate: when the 'ideal' is given historical freedom to experience itself in flesh, in action, we have the tragicomedy of *Nostromo*, we have the Feminine Archetype, Mrs. Gould, at the very center of a storm of mirages, each an 'ideal,' each a masculine fantasy."

"Notes on Failure" is a sympathetic, writer's piece on how failure stimulates art, and how even successful artists always live with the fear of failure. Her shorter pieces, reviews of work by Jean Stafford, Paul Bowles, Flannery O'Connor, Jung, and Anne Sexton, are also fine—generous in spirit and to the point. Perhaps "significantly" (as Oates would say), her bitchiest—and so in many ways her most interesting—review deals with the often revered Simone Weil, whom Oates sees as a self-deluding, self-aggrandizing anorexic. Oates has fascinating things to tell us about the connection between starvation and spurious mystical insight.

Cynthia Ozick puts everything she has into her essays—and that's a lot: wit, fierce intelligence, supple writing, and an absence of hackneyed opinion. Her subjects include literature, Judaism, feminism. Beginning one of her essays, you don't know where it will end up or what strange points she will make along the way. An essay on Truman Capote produces an ironic reminiscence of studying literature at NYU in the post-war years, along with unappreciative Army vets. "Other voices, other rooms—ah, how we felt it, the tug of somewhere else, inchoate, luminous, the enameled radiance of our eternal and gifted youth. Instead, here were these veterans . . . coming alive only for Marketing and Accounting, sniggering at Sheats and Kelley, hating Thomas Wolfe, with every mean money-grubbing diaper-stinking aging bone hating Poetry and Beauty and Transfiguration. . . . Capote was the banner against this blight."

An essay on "Literary Blacks and Jews" proposes that Ralph Ellison, who hunted quail and thanked Hemingway for having written so well about wing shooting, was more at home in America than were Jewish writers such as Bernard Malamud and Irving Howe, with their "bookish moral passion." Ozick, like Oates, writes about "the sacral Updike," but starts with the refreshingly outrageous assumption that we all know he is a "crypto-Christian, a reverse Marrano celebrating the Body of Jesus while hidden inside a bathing suit," and she goes on to rebuke Updike (whose work she loves) for not theologizing his Jewish hero, Henry Bech, as he does his Christian ones. "What passes for Bech-as-Jew is an Appropriate Reference Machine, cranked on whenever Updike reminds himself that he is obligated to produce a sociological symptom: *crank, gnash,* and out flies an inverted sentence."

Ozick's positions are unequivocal and often unfashionable. She dislikes the new feminism which celebrates women's separateness. A classic feminist herself, she hates the term "woman writer" and opposes the idea of a female nature, calling it "the Great Lie." She thinks Jewish writers will last only if they write as Jews and for Jews. Norman Mailer will one day be no more than "a small Gentile footnote." Her deeply religious nature attacks what she calls "idolatry," the worship of anything other than God. And that includes Art. The book concludes with two masterpieces of autobiographical essay, "The Lesson of the Master" and "A Drugstore in Winter," which make very personal the point about idolatry. Her sterile and premature obsession with Henry James postponed her own growth as a writer. She herself was a worshiper of art, an idolater. Her conversion came late, which explains the virulence of her dislike of idolatry. Reading her essays along with those of Oates, who prattles so about the sacredness of Art, one is inclined to see Ozick's point.

SIMONE DE BEAUVOIR

✤ ✤ ✤

A generation of dutiful daughters (myself included) is grateful
to Simone de Beauvoir for *The Second Sex* and *Memoirs of a
Dutiful Daughter*, which were among the few feminist works
available in the 1950s. The heroine of *Memoirs of a Dutiful
Daughter*, the first of what has turned out to be a series of de-
creasingly incisive autobiographies, is a bright middle-class girl,
as obedient as she is ambitious. The book ends on a note of
hope, with the girl in Paris, happily studying for the teaching
degree that will make her independent. She has met Mr. Right
in the person of Jean-Paul Sartre, three years her senior, a future
teacher and writer like herself. They are instant soulmates. She
has her independence and her man. How did it turn out? Can
independence, achievement and intimacy be combined? Was the
twentieth century's greatest literary couple really happy? If so,
how did they do it? *Adieux*, which is partly an account of Sartre's
last ten years and partly a series of conversations between the
two in 1974, answers these questions and more.

De Beauvoir and Sartre were companions for forty-five years,
although they never married and did not live together. De Beauvoir was intensely skeptical about marriage, believing that it was
virtually impossible for a woman who married or even lived with
a man to escape the traditional female role of housekeeper and
caretaker. Sartre and de Beauvoir knew that they would go
through life together and that each would be the most important

✤ *Adieux: A Farewell to Sartre* (New York: Pantheon, 1984) by Simone de
Beauvoir, translated by Patrick O'Brian, and *After "The Second Sex": Con-
versations with Simone de Beauvoir* (New York: Pantheon, 1984) by Alice
Schwarzer, translated by Marianne Howarth.

person in the other's life. But Sartre, an enthusiastic womanizer, made it clear from the beginning that he could not promise fidelity. She, too, had affairs with other men, including the American writer, Nelson Algren. Some people believe de Beauvoir was hurt by Sartre's philandering, which was more frequent and flagrant than her own. I see no sign of it in this book or in her conversations with Alice Schwarzer. Moreover, *Adieux* provides fascinating evidence as to why de Beauvoir might not have cared who Sartre made love with. Apparently, the great existentialist did not much enjoy sex. He liked to touch but not to be touched, and preferred kissing and caressing to "the act of love strictly so called." "I should have been quite happy," he tells de Beauvoir, "naked in bed with a naked woman, caressing and kissing her, but without going as far as the sexual act." As it was, he says, he went through with it because it was expected; he got "a little pleasure at the end, but pretty feeble." One can see why de Beauvoir would not have minded sharing Sartre's "kind of frigidity" with other women, although one would like to know how she felt about being on the receiving end of Sartre's sexual peculiarities. For about two decades they had a sexual relationship; then it ceased. They never stopped talking, however.

Talk, not sex, was the essential bond between them. So it is not surprising that the second and longer part of *Adieux*, the transcripts of their conversations, is vastly more interesting than the first part, de Beauvoir's diarylike memoir of Sartre's final years. The topics of discussion range over Sartre's "relations with" politics, time, women, his own body. We do not get a promised exchange about their relations with each other, but it doesn't matter: the conversations are a kind of enactment of their relationship —and a much better proof of their equality than pages of discursive prose.

I have never read dialogues in which the two speakers are so beautifully matched. What interviewer besides de Beauvoir could have asked Sartre, "When did you lose the stupid notion that

girls who went to bed freely and easily were more or less whores?"
De Beauvoir knows at least as much about Sartre as he does. She
knows, for example, that he is open and friendly to people when
he is sitting in a café but that he will go to any lengths to avoid
asking directions when he's lost. The explanation she forces from
him is revealing: he was reluctant to put himself in a dependent
position, the same avoidance of passivity that made sex so stunted
a business for him. And when he confesses that he was also reluctant to ask directions because it was a kind of imposition and he
was too ugly to impose himself, who but de Beauvoir could reply,
"You're not so ugly that you would make a pregnant woman run
away if you asked her the way to the Rue de Rome."

She lets him get away with little. She points out when he con-
tradicts himself. She helps him tell stories, filling in details. Sometimes she remembers more about his past than he does, and it is
hard to tell who is the interviewer, who the interviewee:

SARTRE: We often slept in the open.

DE BEAUVOIR: Oh, every other night, I think. Without a tent,
without anything. And particularly in that very pretty town near Sparta.
. . . We slept in a church, and when we woke up in the morning there
were all kinds of peasants around us. But I'm the one who is talking; it
ought to be you.

SARTRE: Not at all, we're talking together.

Many people will want to read this book solely for what it
reveals about Sartre. We learn that for twenty years he seriously
abused amphetamines. He was so wired that his feet moved constantly when he sat; his elbows moved so compulsively that he
wore holes in de Beauvoir's armchairs. He took speed to write the
Critique of Dialectical Reason but not to write *The Words*. That
was one of several ways in which he revealed his greater respect
for literature than for philosophy.

Sartre suffered from a lulu of a mind/body split. He believed
that if you're not beautiful, people are predisposed against you.
He got no pleasure from his body and experienced no joy in physi-

cal being. "When I skied, I was mainly afraid of falling," he tells
de Beauvoir. His disdain for the body and sensual pleasure was so
great that one is not surprised to discover there were many things
he didn't like to eat. Crustaceans were distasteful because of their
"doubtful consciousness." He preferred salamis to cooked meat
because the flesh is less evident, and cakes to fruit because there
is more thought in the cake. He was a man who, in every sense,
preferred the cooked to the raw, a living illustration of Lévi-
Straussian polarities. So one is not surprised that, for all his theo-
retical egalitarianism, he believed women were primarily emotional and men primarily rational. Being involved with a woman
was a way of "taking possession of her affectivity."

Sometimes his ability to run his experience through an abstraction machine is quite astounding. Here, for example, Sartre
defends his youthful prank of throwing water bombs:

I believe that when we hid at the top of the stairs in order to throw water
bombs at the boys who came back about midnight wearing dinner jackets
having been dining out, we were thereby indicating that the dining out,
the dinner jacket, the distinguished air, the well-brushed hair, were
wholly exterior things, nonvalues, of no worth.

Elsewhere he explains that he always tried to keep his weight
down "to give the impression of a thin little man instead of a
fat little man." But he can't help adding, "Besides, fatness was
something I thought of as surrender and contingency." Sometimes
de Beauvoir brings him down from these flights. Sometimes she
joins him, and they seem well matched in their humorlessness, as
in so many other qualities.

Sartre was sixty-nine and already failing when these conversations took place (he died in 1980, six years later). Practically
blind, he could not read and could barely write. De Beauvoir
seems to have used the taping of these conversations as a way to
keep him occupied and cheerful. He starts off in low spirits.
"Does this interest you?" she begins the conversations. "At present nothing interests me," he replies. But as she gets him talking

about his past, he begins to come alive. Her effort is touching, as are the moments when she abandons her interviewer's role in order frankly to be a friend and to rouse him from despair:

DE BEAUVOIR: What are your subjective relations to your work as a whole?

SARTRE: I'm not very pleased with it. The novel's a failure.

DE BEAUVOIR: No. It's not finished, but it's not a failure.

SARTRE: Generally speaking, it's been less highly thought of, and I think people are right. As for the philosophical works . . .

DE BEAUVOIR: They're wonderfully good!

SARTRE: Yes, but what do they lead to?

DE BEAUVOIR: I think the *Critique of Dialectical Reason* has advanced thought splendidly!

SARTRE: Isn't it still rather idealistic?

DE BEAUVOIR: I don't think so at all. I believe it can be immensely useful in making the world and people understandable, just like the Flaubert, though in another way . . .

SARTRE: I didn't finish the Flaubert, and I never shall.

DE BEAUVOIR: You haven't finished it. But then the style of *Madame Bovary* wasn't something that interested you all that much.

As can be gauged from that extract, much of the charm of the conversations comes not from their compression or pointedness but from the illusion they convey that we are overhearing authentic speech. Overhearing Sartre and de Beauvoir, you feel a privileged witness to an intimate act.

I confess I could "listen" to these dialogues all day. At times, they remind me of Tom Stoppard, at times of the sparring of lovers in Shakespearean romances. They are found comedy, biographical drama in the raw:

SARTRE: Then there's another thing that gives me pleasure, and that is not having white hair.

DE BEAUVOIR: Your side whiskers are white, and when you don't shave thoroughly your stubble is white too. But since you are sensitive about what ages you, you ought to take more care and shave quite closely. Your hair in fact is gray; it's not white.

SARTRE: It's odd. According to what I've told you I should indeed take care of my person. I should shave better, for instance; and I don't do so. The imaginary character needs a real support, and the support should be as young as possible. There's a contradiction here.

DE BEAUVOIR: Yes, the imaginary character is no doubt slim and lively, whereas the real character has something of a belly. . . . You are not much too fat, but even so, if your fastidiousness matched your imagination you would obviously be thinner.

I don't suppose it will be long before someone puts this on stage.

Although de Beauvoir has gone to considerable trouble throughout her career to portray her relationship with Sartre as ideal, I would like to believe her. Still, it most be acknowledged that he formed a bigger portion of her mental and emotional life than she did of his. Throughout her life, she has talked about him and his work constantly; his work is much less dependent on hers. Were their ages and states of health reversed, I can't imagine him spending time interviewing her or writing books about their relationship after her death. Despite their separate residences, she spent a lot of time and energy taking care of him; he did not take care of her. He was the one who determined the strange sexual character of their relationship.

Without accepting their relationship as ideal or even ideally equal, I can at any rate believe in their happiness, achieved by an unending delight in one another's minds. They traveled together, they listened to music together. One copy of a book served both of them. They played four-handed piano pieces. They criticized each other's work. "I had one special reader," says Sartre, "and that was you. When you said to me, 'I agree; it's all right,' then it was all right. I published the book and I didn't give a damn for the critics. You did me a great service. You gave me a confidence in myself that I should not have had alone." They knew each other's opinions so well that one could speak for both, as when de Beauvoir says, "we" don't like psychoanalysis. Or, as Sartre says in the moving last line of their talks, "We've lived. We feel that we've taken an interest in our world and that we've tried to see and understand it."

The first part of *Adieux*, the chronicle of Sartre's last ten years, is compiled rather than written. The reader is thrown into the complexities of French left-wing politics with no orientation. Throughout, there is the flat recording of judgments typical of uninspired diaries: "One evening Sylvie took us to the opera to hear *The Sicilian Vespers*. . . . The casting was not all that it might have been, but there were some very fine arias and the choruses were splendid. The production, the scenery, and the costumes were outstanding." Details are maddeningly absent: "I questioned [Sartre] on his relations with feminism. He answered with the greatest good will but rather superficially." End of subject. Yet buried in the debris is a poignant document about a man facing death philosophically, observing his body fall apart, worried less about ceasing to exist than about existing in impaired form—worried, for example, that with false teeth, he will no longer be able to speak in public.

To remind myself that there once was a time when Simone de Beauvoir could write, I looked at two earlier works of fiction which have been reissued in paperback by Pantheon: *The Blood of Others*, a 1945 novel, which is being made into a film, and the even more wonderful collection of early stories, *When Things of the Spirit Come First*. Today, de Beauvoir is a better talker than she is a writer. Fair enough. She is seventy-six and has written plenty. Fortunately, her talk is being abundantly recorded.

Her conversations with the West German journalist Alice Schwarzer (collected in *After "The Second Sex"*) took place from 1972 to 1982 and focus on her feminism, which is classic and uncompromising. Her opposition to what she sees as a renaissance of the notion of an innate female nature—a new glorification of motherhood, a new emphasis on femininity—ties the conversations together. Throughout, she expresses herself with freshness and clarity. "Given that one can hardly tell women that washing up saucepans is their divine mission, they are told that bringing up children is their divine mission," she says. "Being a mother these days is real slavery." And "Women are exploited—and they allow themselves to be exploited—in the name of love." Old age is easier for women than for men, she notes, because women have less far to fall. Her continuing message to women is "Be wary." Be wary of marriage, of motherhood, of men. Don't necessarily avoid them, but be careful.

Simone de Beauvoir has led an extraordinary life and she knows it. Despite her intellectual commitment to solidarity with other women, at a deep level she does not seem to feel it. A calm sense of privilege, an air of exemption from the human lot, pervades everything she says. She is certain she has used her intelligence to live better than the rest of us. As a result, we may look up to her, but it's hard to love her. At one point, Schwarzer invites de Beauvoir to identify with other women: "I know quite a few women who have been made to pay for insisting on the right to show their intelligence and strength of character. People around them make them feel: so you are 'as good as any man,' are you? Well, then you are not desirable 'as a woman'! Have you come up against that?" Simone de Beauvoir's answer? "No."

THE CASE OF
WILLA CATHER

✤ ✤ ✤

In the 1950s David Daiches cannily predicted that literary historians would have difficulty placing Willa Cather. He did not foresee that Cather's work would be underrated because it was hard to place, but such may have been the case. You could say that Cather has been ignored because she was a woman, but that would not explain why her rediscovery has taken ten years longer than Virginia Woolf's. Generally perceived as a traditionalist, Cather has been patronized. Many people read her for pleasure, but for the past twenty years few have taught her works or written about them. The novels seem curiously self-evident. Smooth and elegant, they lack the rough edges that so often provide convenient starting points for literary analysis. To a critical tradition that has valued complexity, ambiguity, even obscurity, the hard-won simplicities of Cather's art seem merely simple. Her lucidity can be read as shallowness; her massive, abstract forms can be—and have been—viewed as naïvely traditional, the appropriate vehicle for an art essentially nostalgic and elegiac.

Although I distrust the way in which, for twentieth-century writers, the term "modernist" is not merely an honorific but the precondition of attention from literary critics and scholars, I will nonetheless try to show ways in which Willa Cather's work is allied to modernism. I do this by way of redressing a balance. Her public stance was so belligerently reactionary (perhaps in order to mask the radically unacceptable nature of her private life) that she encouraged the flattening of her work into a glorification of the past, a lament for the shabbiness of the present, which has persisted for decades. The writer who titled a collection of essays

Not Under Forty would not have felt congratulated to be called a modernist. But it is time to risk her wrath. In part because of her defensive self-presentation, in part because her fiction so perfectly embodies certain aesthetic ideals of modernism, we have overlooked its innovative nature. Her work is moved in important ways by a modernist urge to simplify and to suggest the eternal through the particular. Because we have paid more attention to other aspects of literary modernism—the overtly experimental, the representation of subjectivity, the literary analogues of cubist collage—we react to Cather's novels as though we have stumbled across some giant work of nature, a boulder, something so massive that it seems inhuman, uncrafted. But I would suggest that what we have stumbled upon in fact is something like the literary equivalent of an Arp, a Brancusi, a Moore.

I would point first of all to her scale. I do not mean the size of her books, for they are little masterpieces of economy; I mean the size of the subjects to which her imagination responds. In her strongest work, the land is as much a presence as the human characters, and the landscapes that move her imagination are large and unbroken ones. The vast Nebraska prairie, which Cather saw for the first time when she was ten, transplanted from the hill-enclosed perspectives of Virginia, determined—or answered to—her sense of scale. The impact of the prairie on her sense of self was probably such as her narrative stand-in, Jim Burden, describes in *My Ántonia*: "There seemed to be nothing to see; no fences, creeks, or trees, no hills or fields. . . . I had the feeling that the world was left behind, that we had got over the edge of it, and were outside men's jurisdiction. I had never before looked up at the sky when there was not a familiar mountain ridge against it. But this was the complete dome of heaven, all there was of it . . . Between that earth and that sky I felt erased, blotted out." To feel "erased, blotted out" is not, from Cather's perspective, such a bad thing. The scale of the landscape erases trivialities of personality. In one of the most beautiful passages in American literature, Cather presents Jim in his grandmother's garden, resting his back against a sun-warmed pumpkin, his individuality transcended. "I was something that lay under the sun and felt it, like the pumpkins, and I did not want to be anything more. I was entirely happy. Perhaps we feel like that when we die and become part of something entire, whether it is sun and air, or goodness and knowledge. At any rate, that is happiness; to be dissolved into something complete and great."

Against the background of the plains, only the biggest stories stand out—stories based on the most elemental emotions. "There are only two or three human stories," Cather wrote in *O Pioneers!*, "and they go on repeating themselves as fiercely as if they had never happened before." If you approach *O Pioneers!* as a naturalistic account of the conquest of new land, four-fifths of the book is irrelevant, and you must wonder why the story of the adulterous love of Emil Bergson and Marie Shabata and their murder by her jealous husband is taking up so much space in a book about pioneers. In fact, the love of Emil and Marie is the focus of the story. As in ballads, motivation is played down; motives in such oft-enacted human stories are assumed to speak for themselves.

In the American Southwest, which Cather visited for the first time in 1912, she found not only another monumental landscape but the temporal equivalent for the vast spaces of the Midwest. For these were not uninhabited spaces whose history was just beginning. The great half-dome caverns on the cliff-sides of canyons contained the remains of an ancient, civilized people. Cliff-dwelling Indians had lived, cultivated the land, and produced art, long before Europeans had landed on American soil. The long-inhabited, long-abandoned monumental landscape lengthened the past. If you included the Indians, American history, which had seemed so small and cramped a thing, suddenly became vast.

Cather's books repeatedly struggle to break outside the confines of town or city life and make their way, quite against the grain of the narrative, back to the wilderness. *The Song of the Lark* gets to Panther Canyon by way of the unlikely premise that Thea Kronborg, studying music in Chicago, needs the experience of that locale to change her from a good artist into a great one. The effect of the canyonland on her sense of herself is like the effect of the prairie on Jim Burden: it obliterates the trivial and raises her, spiritually, to its own scale.

Tom Outland's story of the discovery of the cliff-dweller ruins on the Blue Mesa bears an even more tenuous plot connection to the rest of *The Professor's House*, which concerns a transitional crisis in the life of a midwestern university professor. In the sudden, eccentric switch to the southwestern locale, we witness a Catherian compulsion. Explaining it, however, as an experiment in form, Cather said she wanted to reproduce the effect of a square window opening into a distant prospect in a Dutch genre painting. She said she wanted the reader first to stifle amidst the trappings of American bourgeois domesticity, then to feel the clean air blowing in from the mesa.* But the effect of the massive dislocation within *The Professor's House* is less like the effect of Dutch genre painting, which carefully subordinates one scale to the other, than it is like the effect of surrealism, with its willful changes of scale and its reminders, within a canvas, of the artificiality of the canvas—Magritte's painting of a view out the window blocked by a painting of a view out the window, or Charles Sheeler's ironic *The Artist Looks at Nature*, which depicts Sheeler out-of-doors, painting a kitchen interior. Cather inserts the outdoors into the indoors as willfully as Sheeler's self-portrait does the reverse, justifying the change however she can.

The pattern in *The Song of the Lark* and *The Professor's House* is repeated in her work as a whole. She alternates between two modes—a more conventional realism, which is evoked when she

* Willa Cather, "On *The Professor's House*," in *Willa Cather on Writing* (New York: Knopf, 1949), p. 31.

sets herself the task of describing people in groups, living in houses, and a more abstract and lyrical mode, evoked by people against a landscape. Writing about indoor people—Thea Kronborg, Bartley Alexander, Godfrey St. Peter—she writes in small strokes, with more circumstantial detail, with more accounts of what people think and say. Her first novel, *Alexander's Bridge*, was in this mode and has always reminded readers of the work of Henry James and Edith Wharton. Later, Cather preferred to think of *O Pioneers!* as her first novel, because it was the one in which she discovered the lyrical mode that she considered her authentic style. It is the mode in which her best books—*My Ántonia*, and *Death Comes for the Archbishop* as well as *O Pioneers!*—are written. Deeply associated with it, perhaps necessary to generate it, is the quality I have been calling scale.

Heroic simplification is the essence of Cather's approach to character. We are first introduced to Alexandra Bergson, for example, through the eyes of a traveling salesman whose sole function is to provide a perspective on the heroine. And what does he think of her? That she is "a fine human creature" who makes him wish he was more of a man. That is, she makes an impact without individuation. Although Alexandra has a good deal of character —she is placid, firm, in some ways a visionary—Cather's presentation of her consists of broad strokes. Alexandra is not clever in the manner of city-bred and well-educated people, such as the characters Cather had written about in *Alexander's Bridge*; and that absence of cleverness allowed—perhaps forced—Cather to treat character in a new way in *O Pioneers!*. Alexandra cannot be an interesting "center of consciousness" in a Jamesian sense, because her consciousness is insufficiently complex. Nor is it the most important part of her. Her conscious mind is a "white book, with clear writing about weather and beasts and growing things. Not many people would have cared to read it." So we see her resolutely from the outside, and this, along with Cather's persistent contrast of her in terms of size to those around her ("'What a hopeless position you are in, Alexandra!' [Carl] exclaimed feverishly. 'It is your fate to be always surrounded by little men'"), creates the illusion of grandeur which is a distinguishing trait of Cather's heroines.

For Jamesian centers of consciousness, Cather substitutes objects of admiration. Her favorite narrator is the adoring young person, usually a man, creating out of some woman a creature with mythic resonance: Jim Burden and Ántonia, Neil Herbert and Marian Forrester in A Lost Lady, also Nellie Birdseye and Myra Henshawe in My Mortal Enemy. Ántonia provides the best example, for she is not so much characterized as mythicized from the opening to the conclusion: "She lent herself to immemorial attitudes which we recognize by instinct as universal and true. . . . She had only to stand in the orchard, to put her hand on a little crab tree and look up at the apples, to make you feel the goodness of planting and tending and harvesting at last. . . . She was a rich mine of life, like the founders of early races." Ántonia is more a goddess of fertility than an individuated woman.

Cather shared the impatience with individuated character that she saw reflected in the way southwestern Indians spoke English or Spanish, dropping the definite articles: not "the mountain" but "mountain"; not "the woman" but "woman." She often presents her characters as conduits for a divine spirit, raised above human powers by some force above or below consciousness, approaching the condition of gods, goddesses, or saints. Archbishop Latour could easily have been made to seem a cathedral-building, executive, and managerial paragon. We see him first when he is lost in the desert, identifying with Christ's agony on the cross. From then on, his "story" is largely a record of his finding or losing the spirit of God. Cather repeatedly chooses artists as subjects because she has an archaic sense of the way, in performing or creating, they are possessed by divine inspiration that blows away consciousness of the petty circumstances of their lives.

Cather's art is peculiarly keen at registering surges of energy and at noting the presence or absence of spirit—in an innocent girl like Lucy Gayheart or in an amoral woman like Marian Forrester, who resembles Lucy only in that she puts her whole heart into everything she does. Indeed, most of Cather's heroines— Lucy, Marian, Ántonia, and Alexandra—have the capacity, sometimes harmful to themselves, to live so intensely that they seem like powers more than people. Cather seems sometimes to have set herself the task of portraying pure spirit divorced from circumstance. Background and circumstance seem merely accidents, and, in the earth-mother Ántonia as in the bitchy, bitter Myra Henshawe, what seems essential is the vital breath. Although she would have been appalled by the terms "blood knowledge" and "head knowledge," Cather resembles Lawrence in her desire to bypass the conscious and intellectual elements in her characters in quest of the instinctual and unconscious. These elements she found most accessible in simple people like the farmers of the Divide, in the devout, like the Old World Catholics of her later books, or, in their ideal imagined form, Indians. (When Mabel Dodge married Tony Luhan, a Taos Indian, and many of her friends asked how she could do it, Willa Cather reportedly said, "How could she not?")

But if Cather and Lawrence were in some sense after the same thing in their characters, they went about it in very different ways, and she attacks him as a mere cataloguer of physical sensations and emotions in her most important critical statement, "The Novel Démeublé." Most of this essay is a rather predictable attack on the novel of physical realism, which she calls "over-furnished," overly devoted to description and observation. Balzac serves as her example of misguided labor, as Bennett, Wells, and Galsworthy served in Virginia Woolf's comparable manifestos, "Modern Fiction" and "Mr. Bennett and Mrs. Brown." Balzac, says Cather, wanted to put the city of Paris on paper, with all its houses, upholstery, games of chance and pleasure, even its foods.

This was a mistake, she believes. "The things by which he still lives, the types of greed and avarice and ambition and vanity and lost innocence of heart which he created—are as vital today as they were then. But their material surroundings, upon which he expended such labor and pains . . . the eye glides over them." *

At this point Cather moves away from Woolf, who rejected physical realism in favor of psychological realism, outer for inner, and moves instead toward an aesthetic of the archetypal, toward Jung rather than Freud. She asserts that it is possible to be materialistic about the inner life as well as the outer and offers Lawrence as example. Cataloguing sensations, he robs the great stories of their intrinsic grandeur. "Can one imagine anything more terrible than the story of *Romeo and Juliet* rewritten in prose by D. H. Lawrence?" * The minds of one's characters can be overfurnished, too.

In her insistence on presenting her characters from the outside, Cather seems to fly most conspicuously in the face of modernism, but that is because we have overidentified modernism in the novel with the techniques of interior monologue and stream of consciousness. Interior monologue and Cather's resolutely external treatment are equally reactions against traditional characterization. If we posit a traditional method of characterization in which the inner expresses itself in the outer—both action and physical surroundings—in which character is compassable, knowable, and if we think of this as a middle-distance shot, then interior monologue may be thought of as a close-up, emphasizing uniqueness and individuality to the point of unknowability, and Cather's method of characterization as a kind of long shot, emphasizing the archetypal and eternally human, acknowledging individuality, perhaps, but not exploring it. Joyce tried to incorporate both the close-up and the long shot in his presentation of Leopold Bloom by suggesting that this highly individuated man was an avatar of

* *Willa Cather on Writing*, pp. 38–39.
* *Willa Cather on Writing*, p. 42.

Odysseus; Virginia Woolf seems to want to present eternal types in *The Waves* and to some extent in *Between the Acts*; and Lawrence likes to show his characters in the grip of cosmic forces, wrenched away from the personal. By abandoning the attempt to represent interior consciousness, Cather in her own way participated in the attempt to render the generally human. This is what I mean by the urge to abstraction in her handling of character: her downplaying of individuality, her lack of interest in "personality" as opposed to essential force.

Naïve readers responding to *O Pioneers!* or *My Ántonia* or *Death Comes for the Archbishop* have trouble seeing these works as novels. They appear to be collections of vignettes or sketches, and the connection between the parts is not always evident. This response is useful, reminding us how unconventional Cather's approach to form is. Except in *The Song of the Lark*, her most traditional novel, Cather pays no more attention to plot than Woolf does in *To the Lighthouse* and looks for unity to mood. "It is hard now to realize how revolutionary in form *My Ántonia* was at that time in America," wrote Edith Lewis, Cather's companion. "It seemed to many people to have no form." *

In the first part of *My Ántonia*, for example, one comes suddenly upon a story so powerful that it threatens to throw the novel off track: the story of Pavel and Peter, who, back in Russia, had been carrying a bride and groom home from their wedding in a sled over snow by moonlight, when the entire party was set upon by wolves. To lighten their load and make it to safety, Pavel and Peter throw the bride out of the sled to be devoured by the wolves. At first this violent, horrific story seems separate from the novel as a whole, but with time one's mind weaves it into the fabric. It serves as a prologue to the grim winter. And in the sacrifice of the bride so that Pavel and Peter may reach the safety of town, the story states, with the starkness of folktale, the theme

* Edith Lewis, *Willa Cather Living* (New York: Knopf, 1953), p. 107.

of sexuality sacrificed to advancement which is the heart of the book. But the real power of the story comes from our awareness that Pavel and Peter are ordinary men whose lives had once been suddenly shifted into the realm of elemental forces, then dropped back down again into the ordinary, men metaphorically struck by lightning who go back the next day—or the next month—to milking cows. The narrative exemplifies the way in which Cather's fiction moves between the quotidian and the elemental, acknowledging the abrupt transformations of the ordinary into the ghastly or transcendent.

Other writers, hardly modernists, have used inset stories—Cervantes and Dickens, for example. But in Cather the folktale material is not framed by the rest of the narrative; it penetrates it, bringing what might be read merely as naturalistic narrative into the realm of the mythic, so that, later in the novel, we are aesthetically prepared, though still surprised and shocked, when a tramp wanders in from the prairie, climbs onto a threshing machine, waves his hand gaily, and jumps head first into the blades. Why should a tramp be immune to despair? Heroic emotions are not just for heroes. Cather routinely works with mythic incident (Jim's killing of the giant rattlesnake), with folk material, and with dreams. Naturalism coexists with symbolism. Lena Lingard may be an upwardly mobile, sexy, independent dressmaker in Lincoln, Nebraska, when Jim is a student there, but she is at the same time what she appears to him in a dream: a woman in a wheat field with a scythe, both a symbol of harvest and a figure threatening death, the pleasant death of his will and ambition by surrender to her compelling sensuality.

With such an emphasis on the timeless, with the way in which human beings embody recurrent impulses and attitudes, with Swedish immigrant girls in Nebraska as avatars of Virgilian rustics, no wonder *My Ántonia* defies traditional temporal organization, plot. Dorothy Van Ghent has noted how, out of homely American detail, Cather composes in *My Ántonia* "certain friezelike entablatures that have the character of ancient ritual and sculpture." * "The suffering of change, the sense of irreparable loss in time, is one polarity of the work; the other polarity is the timelessness of those images associated with Ántonia, with the grave of the suicide at the crossroads, with the mute fortitude of the hired men and the pastoral poetry of the hired girls, and most of all with the earth itself." In appreciating Cather's instinct for the timeless, Van Ghent begins to see the implications in formal terms of that instinct, the "frieze-like entablatures," the sculptural and abstract forms throughout Cather's work. "The boldest and most beautiful of Willa Cather's fictions are characterized by a sense of the past not as an irrecoverable quality of events, wasted in history, but as persistent human truths—salvaged, redeemed— by virtue of memory and art." †

Most critics have noticed only the nostalgia, the "sense of irreparable loss in time" in Cather's work, and that leads them to misperceive her art as traditional. To Leon Edel, for example, *Death Comes for the Archbishop* is an exercise in nostalgia, signaling Cather's final retreat into the past. That, indeed, is the way most critics of the forties and fifties—all dominated by a moralistic response to Cather, all disposed to condemn her for retreating into the past, all viewing her as a traditionalist—saw that book.

In fact, from a formal point of view, *Death Comes for the Archbishop*, that extraordinary compilation of vivid scenes and great stories which ignores chronological time, is the most daring and innovative of Cather's works. It perfectly embodies the antiillusionist aesthetic which many of her early books strove for. I

---

* Dorothy Van Ghent, *Willa Cather*, University of Minnesota Pamphlets on American Writers, no. 36 (Minneapolis: University of Minnesota Press, 1964), p. 23. Like just about everything Van Ghent wrote, this is an inspired piece of literary criticism and the best short appreciation of Cather that exists.

† Ibid., p. 5.

will quote Cather's own excellent description of what she was trying to accomplish:

I had all my life wanted to do something in the style of legend, which is absolutely the reverse of dramatic treatment. Since I first saw the Puvis de Chavannes frescoes of the life of St. Genevieve in my student days, I have wished that I could try something a little like that in prose; something without accent, with none of the artificial elements of composition. In the Golden Legend the martyrdoms of the saints are no more dwelt upon than are the trivial incidents of their lives; it is as though all human experiences, measured against one supreme spiritual experience, were of about the same importance. The essence of such writing is not to hold the note, not to use an incident for all there is in it—but to touch and pass on. I felt that such writing would be a discipline in these days when the "situation" is made to count for so much in writing, when the general tendency is to force things up. In this kind of writing the mood is the thing—all the little figures and stories are mere improvisations that come out of it.*

The distinctive note of modernism appears in her aspiration to do "something without accent," in her impatience with "artificial elements of composition," with traditional climaxes and resolutions ("not a single button sewn on as the Bond Street tailors would have it," said Virginia Woolf).† Musically speaking, this lifelong lover of opera repudiates the operatic ("holding the note") as a model for fiction and turns instead—rather astonishingly—to jazz, with its emphasis on mood-generated "improvisations."

The attempt to write "something in the style of legend" involved the pursuit of another aesthetic quality: anonymity. This was hard for Cather to achieve. She had been a high school teacher; more important, she had suffered in her youth from the disapproval of her community, who regarded her nonconformity with distaste. She could never quite stop telling them off for it, and the theme

* *Willa Cather on Writing*, pp. 9–10.
† Virginia Woolf, "Modern Fiction," in *Collected Essays*, 4 vols. (New York: Harcourt, Brace & World, 1967), 2, 106.

of opposition between philistine materialism and artistic dedication too often evokes a marring didacticism in her work. The way
she overcame the urge to preach was by complete submission to
her material. And when she suppressed herself, she did it more
completely than any writer I can think of.

The clarity and simplicity—the sheer absence of eccentricity—
of Cather's prose style contributes to the effect of anonymity. She
adheres to the traditional structure of the English sentence—subject, verb, object—as the surest way of suppressing individuality.
Rarely does one find any complicated syntax. There are passages
in Cather's writing that stop the heart with their beauty, but they
are never purple passages in the usual sense. They tend, as in this
passage, to depict moments of quiet, and they are signaled, if at
all, by a toning down of the prose rather than a keying up.

Far up above me, a thousand feet or so, set in a great cavern in the face
of the cliff, I saw a little city of stone, asleep. It was as still as sculpture—
and something like that. It all hung together, seemed to have a kind of
composition; pale little houses of stone nestling close to one another,
perched on top of each other, with flat roofs, narrow windows, straight
walls, and in the middle of the group, a round tower. . . . It was red in
colour, even on that grey day. In sunlight it was the colour of winter oak-
leaves. A fringe of cedars grew along the edge of the cavern, like a
garden. They were the only living things. Such silence and stillness and
repose—immortal repose. That village sat looking down into the canyon
with the calmness of eternity. [*The Professor's House*]

Although the moment Cather describes here is characteristic—
the small and particular raised to the monumental, the once-busy
seen in eternal repose—the force of this passage resides as much
in its style, in the calm, methodical notation of colors and shapes,
the note of awe suggested with no overtones of hysteria, as in its
content. It insists on the sculptural qualities of its subject, as
Cather tends to in her descriptions of prairie and sky as well. The
prose is by no means flowery, but neither is it as stark as it might
be, as Hemingway's is, for example. A softness comes from Cath-

er's willingness to offer neutral elaboration. "In the sunlight it was the colour of winter oak-leaves"—this is a nice detail but not hypercharged, as it might appear in Hemingway, where the excessively stripped-down quality of the prose makes everything seem almost too significant. Cather's range is more comfortable, and the effect is to reduce, symbolically, the glare. Georgia O'Keeffe comes to mind, as opposed to Dali or Magritte.

O'Keeffe, Sheeler, and other visual artists allied, however loosely, with Precisionism in America offer a good example of aesthetic urges similar to Cather's, generated from analogous but different sources and worked out quite independently. The aim of the Precisionists was simplification of form, and this joined an impulse towards monumentalizing ordinary objects—Sheeler's *Totems in Steel*, for example, a rendering of steel girders on a building project, or his eerie stairwells or imperious ladder-back chairs, or O'Keeffe's resonant adobe houses. Cather particularly recalls O'Keeffe in her response to the Southwest, in her homage to the scale of the American landscape, in her ability to monumentalize the ordinary, and in her gift for generating a sense of mystery out of simplified forms.* Cather's sources of inspiration invite comparison with Sheeler's. Sheeler's formalism fed on a deeply native tradition which was not in itself modernist: he was a student of Shaker furniture and Shaker barns. Similarly, Cather took strength from what she saw as a native example of functionalism, the stories of Sarah Orne Jewett. In describing Jewett's work, Cather distinguished between two kinds of beauty: the beauty of the

* The thrill of the native discovery of abstraction is recorded—so ecstatically as to verge on the comic—in the Daybooks of Edward Weston, particularly in those sections dealing with his 1930 photographs of peppers: "Twenty years of effort . . . have gone into the making of this pepper, which I consider a peak of achievement. It is classic, completely satisfying—a pepper—but more than a pepper: abstract, in that it is completely outside subject matter. It has no psychological attributes, no human emotions are aroused: this new pepper takes one beyond the world we know in the conscious mind." *Edward Weston: The Flame of Recognition*, ed. Nancy Newhall (Millerton, N. Y.: Aperture Monograph, 1975), p. 34.

Chinese junk, which comes from ornamentation and embellishment, and the beauty of the racing yacht, in which every line is subsumed to purpose. Although it is possible to imagine a stripping down and functionalism that goes well beyond Cather's—Hemingway, again—that is certainly the beauty she aspired to herself.

Every great writer is an innovator, forging his or her own style in the face of the seductive force of the conventional. We must mean more than that when we use the term "modernist." Critics of the sixties tended to identify modernism in the novel with subjectivity, but newer accounts of modernism tend to emphasize art's awareness of its own artificial status. The modernists themselves, however, did not unanimously recognize that what they were producing was semiotically precocious fiction; nor were all of them effective theorists of their own positions. Joyce talked about the artist refined out of existence. Eliot talked about art as an escape from personality. Flaubert aspired to write a novel about nothing. Woolf talked about capturing the luminous halo of life. In this company, Cather, with her talk of the "novel *démeublé*," seems the least critically sophisticated, yet it is certainly in this company that she belongs. In modernist critical writings, including Cather's, certain themes recur: an urge to shake loose of clutter, a refusal to accept the mimetic function of art as previously defined, a feeling that a certain "spirit" was escaping the older forms, an urge towards anonymity. The vessel is emphasized rather than the content; art is imagined as a fragile container for the ineffable substance of life. The modernists were aware of art as created artifact, not as a mirror reflecting reality or a camera eye absorbing and imprinting it. Often, like Cather, they looked to Flaubert as their Ur-aesthetician, with his emphasis on style, surface, disciplined craft; but the wittiest theorist of modernism was Oscar Wilde, whose assertion that life imitates art may be seen as the key to the modernist spirit.

If we describe the modernists as self-conscious artificers who rejected mimesis, we risk overemphasizing the intellectual, game-playing, Nabokovian element in modernism. Not all experiment took place for the sake of experiment, but out of a conviction that the old forms did not capture something important in life, a "spirit," a force, a religious or spiritual dimension existing somewhere below or above consciousness but beyond the purviews of traditional fiction. Hence modernism's impatience with describing the here-and-now and its persistent urge to see the here-and-now in the light of, united to, all of human history.

An interest in the past and particularly in primitive cultures characterized the early twentieth century and was not just a piece of isolated nostalgia or conservatism on the part of Willa Cather. Gauguin had been impressed by Aztec sculpture at the Paris Exposition as early as 1889. Vlaminck began collecting African sculpture around 1903 and was followed in his enthusiasm for primitive art by Derain, Matisse, Modigliani, Brancusi, Moore, and Picasso, who, in 1907, incorporated renderings of African sculptures into Les Demoiselles d'Avignon. Picasso had visited Altamira in 1902 to see the neolithic cave paintings. Lawrence left the Old World for the New in search of more ancient civilizations.

The same impulse drove Cather to Walnut Canyon, Arizona, and later to Mesa Verde, where she found in the buildings and pottery of the Anasazi an objective correlative for aesthetic impulses she had felt in herself. Form in these cliff dwellings followed function; the buildings blended with the landscape; towns were set inside natural caverns with the cliffs themselves providing protection from the elements. The pottery was elegantly functional, embellished only with abstract designs. No more in these designs than in Indian pictographs, no more than in the cave paintings of Altamira or in certain Greek vase painting, was there an attempt to imitate three-dimensionality on a flat surface. It is no surprise that a woman so moved by this art should

also have responded strongly to the frescoes of Puvis de Chavannes, with their flat, almost friezelike figures. Although Puvis
de Chavannes was not himself a modernist figure, he influenced
Seurat, Gauguin, Matisse, and Picasso. Most modern painting has
stemmed from a refusal like his to create the illusion of three-
dimensional space, often encouraged by the example of primitive, non-Western, or pre-Renaissance art. Cather's antinatural-
istic *Death Comes for the Archbishop*, a series of stories so
arranged as to blur the distinction between the past and the
present, the miraculous and the mundane, is, I would argue, a true
even if somewhat surprising example in literature of the modernist
aesthetic in art.

However fragmented their initial impact, both *The Waste Land*
and *Ulysses* attempt to transcend the complexity of modern life
by mobilizing the structural simplicities of myth. The appropriate
stance for the artist in the face of such an enterprise is anonymity.
The appropriate style is no style. Joyce in *Ulysses* sought to ap-
proximate "no style" by parodying all styles. Gertrude Stein and
Hemingway sought to produce an anonymous surface by means
of prose styles of the utmost plainness, stripped of all ornament
and connotation. But the lucid prose of Willa Cather makes even
Hemingway's sentences look mannered. And as for Gertrude Stein,
it is one of the many ironies of modernism that the pursuit of simplicity and anonymity produced works of such futile complexity
and obtrusive personality. Like many other modernist artists,
Cather sought to bypass consciousness and the circumstantial details with which it concerns itself and to produce an art that ap-
pealed to the most elemental layers of our minds. Her enduring
popularity with readers shows that she succeeded, and critics
ought now to take account of her success.

INDEX

✦ ✦ ✦

Crossing Brooklyn Ferry (Whitman), 71
Cummings, E. E., 28

Daiches, David, 136
Death Comes for the Archbishop
   (Cather), 17, 140, 144, 146, 152
Death of a Salesman (Miller), 80
de Beauvoir, Simone, see Beauvoir,
   Simone de
Deceased Dimas, The (Kahlo), 24
Demoiselles d'Avignon, Les
   (Picasso), 151
Deutsch, André, 106
"Dialogues for One Voice"
   (Colette), 94
Diane Arbus: A Biography (Bos-
   worth), 60–63
Dickens, Charles, 8, 109, 145
Dickinson, Emily, 48
Dickinson, Violet, 117
Difficult Women: A Memoir of Three
   (Plante), 102–3
Dinesen, Isak (Baroness Karen
   Blixen-Finecke), 6, 12, 40–45
   American audience of, 44–45
   Finch Hatton's affair with, 40,
      42–43
   marriage of, 40, 42
   sexual sacrifice of, 40, 41
   as storyteller, 40–41
   syphilis contracted by, 40, 42
Djuna: The Life and Times of Djuna
   Barnes (Field), 28–34
Doctorow, E. L., 77–78, 80
Dostoevsky, Fyodor, 98
Doyle, Peter, 73
Drabble, Margaret, 13, 109–14
   as chronicler of contemporary
      Britain, 109–10, 112–14
   early novels of, 109
   psychological characterizations
      of, 110–11
   Woolfian or Proustian reveries
      of, 111–12
"Drugstore in Winter, A" (Ozick),
   127
Duke of Deception, The (Woolf), 67

Edel, Leon, 74, 146
Eden, Emily, 13, 115–18
   family life of, 116–18
   letters of, 116–17
   pithy characterizations of, 116
Eden, Fanny, 117
Eden, George, Lord Auckland, 117
Eden, Mrs. William, Lady Auckland,
   117
Eden, William, Lord Auckland, 117
Eliot, George (Mary Ann Evans), 7,
   65, 68, 77
Eliot, T. S., 28–29, 150
   Woolf's letters to, 87
Ellison, Ralph, 126
Ellmann, Mary, 11
Eminent Victorians (Strachey), 75
English Institute, 5–6
Executioner's Song, The (Mailer),
   78–80

Faber & Faber, 29
family biography, 67
Father and Son (Gosse), 67
Faulkner, William, 70
feminine style, 8, 9–10
   masculine style vs., 8, 9–10, 18–19
feminism, 3, 5, 9, 10–11, 27, 41, 69
   of Beauvoir, 134–35
   Drabble on, 112
   of Franklin, 121–22
   of Ozick, 127
feminist biography, 27, 29
Field, Andrew, 28–34
   Barnes overly praised by, 28–30
   Barnes victimized by, 33–34
   as innovative biographer, 32
Finch Hatton, Denys, 40, 42–43
Flaubert, Gustav, 85, 89, 96, 132, 150
Ford, Ford Madox, 99, 100
Forty Days of Musa Dagh, The
   (Werfel), 54
Franklin, Miles, 119–23
   Brent of Bin Bin as pseudonym of,
      122
   literary success of, 121
   My Brilliant Career, 119–21
   reform work and philanthropy of,
      121–22, 123